The Courage
to Fail

The Courage to Fail

Art Mortell's Secrets
for Business Success

Art Mortell

McGraw-Hill, Inc.
New York   San Francisco   Washington, D.C.   Auckland   Bogotá
Caracas   Lisbon   London   Madrid   Mexico City   Milan
Montreal   New Delhi   San Juan   Singapore
Sydney   Tokyo   Toronto

Library of Congress Cataloging-in-Publication Data

Mortell, Art.
    The courage to fail : Art Mortell's secrets for business success / Art Mortell.
        p.   cm.
    Includes index.
    ISBN 0-07-043392-5 (hc)
    1. Success in business. I. Title.
    HF5386.M775   1993
    650.1—dc20

                                    92-26435
                                      CIP

1 2 3 4 5 6 7 8 9 0 DOC/DOC 9 8 7 6 5 4 3 2

ISBN   0-07-043392-5

The sponsoring editor for this book was Betsy N. Brown, the editing supervisor was John Fitzpatrick of Editorial Services of New England, and the production supervisor was Suzanne W. Babeuf. This book was set in Palatino by McGraw-Hill's Professional Book Group composition unit.

Printed and bound by R. R. Donnelley & Sons Company.

To everyone who has ever taken failure and rejection personally, become depressed, and yet had the courage to confront their fear, develop their potential and enhance their self-esteem

About the Author

Art Mortell is president of Systematic Achievement, a
Malibu, California–based consulting firm. For the past 25
years, he has been an internationally recognized speaker to
many of America's largest and most innovative companies,
and he presents seminars to approximately 200 groups each
year. He is the author of the highly praised *World Class
Selling*.

Contents

Preface

We all want to become financially successful, gain recognition and be emotionally satisfied. Unfortunately, many of us experience the opposite. We are in a period of adversity, confronting negative feedback and stress.

Too often, when people experience failure, rejection and anxiety, they quit. Rather than follow an adventurous path, they seek the path of least resistance. While they might be quite comfortable in their predictable lives, what's missing is the excitement that comes capitalizing on existing opportunities and increasing self-respect. Truly exceptional people constantly strive to succeed and, during difficult times, excel.

We benefit more from failure than success. Adversity challenges us to accelerate the development of our greatest potential. Reacting decisively to rejection strengthens our self-image and disengages resistance. Then negative feedback only serves to stimulate us, and provides an opportunity to improve our persuasive skills. Soon the hostility of others is completely disarmed by our relentless compassion.

If we do not change our attitude toward failure and our reactions to rejection, we will become frustrated and experience emotional pain. The only way out of this impasse is to understand how to channel anxiety into a creative force for achievement. We must replace the self-destructive addictions that people use to cope with stress with positive addictions for thriving on anxiety.

Gradually failure will become a catalyst for success, rejection an instrument for raising our self-esteem and anxiety a productive energy for achievement. We capitalize on the opportunities, we multiply our talents and achieve our high expectations.

The *Courage to Fail* provides a blueprint for guiding us through life's most stressful situations. You will be inspired by the real-life experiences of people who have risen above their failures and used rejection to catapult them to even greater heights. My hope is that these principles, which have helped thousands achieve high expectations, will help you reach new levels of financial success and personal satisfaction.

Acknowledgments

My thanks to all those people who contributed their personal experiences of persevering through disappointment, negative feedback and stressful situations. In particular, I appreciate the efforts of my friend, Steve Drozdeck, who initiated this project; Betsy Brown, my editor, who believed in the value of the concepts; Ted Nardin, whose guidelines significantly improved the substance of the book; George Seldin, whose creative management ability effectively directed the development of the material; Jay Klahn, whose critical insight focused the ideas; and Deborah Mallonee, whose perspectives personalized the concepts of the manuscript. Special thanks to Mom, who made so many corrections.

Art Mortell

1

Failure, Always a Beneficial Experience

1

Achieving
High
Expectations

> We begin to succeed when we learn how to fail.

In 1961 I received my college degree. I felt as though I had traveled through a passageway that had taken me from childhood to the threshold of adulthood. With high expectations I was ready to achieve something significant and become financially independent. Yet my determination to excel was mixed with vague feelings of apprehension. I knew where I wanted to go, but how was I going to get there? It was as though I had a destination without a road map.

As I explored many occupations, I realized a career as a teacher or social worker lacked the challenge and financial opportunity I wanted. The more research I did, the more convinced I became that selling was the solution. In a sales position I would be forced to become self-disciplined, confident and persuasive. I also wanted to be a professional person in a prestigious job. How could I do both? I decided the answer was selling for IBM. Their reputation in the marketplace was outstanding, and their training program was excellent.

My initial interview with IBM seemed positive, and I felt I had done reasonably well. However, the manager did not hire me because I lacked business experience. Traveling back to Brooklyn on the subway, I was not particularly disappointed. His decision was understandable, and the solution was obvious. I would have to get the required experience.

Within a few days I was hired by Old Town Corporation, a manufacturer of office supplies. My responsibilities included everything from advertising to sales promotion. As the months passed, I became more aware of how a company's success is based on sales productivity. If I could succeed in selling, I would increase my value to the company, so I asked for a sales territory.

My boss, the vice president of sales, was amused by my request. He looked out the window and pointed to the Williamsburg Savings Bank building. "Art," he explained, "that's the biggest building in Brooklyn, and the salesman who has this territory will not mind if you were to experiment. Good luck."

The next morning I began contacting prospective clients and discussing products such as carbon paper and typewriter ribbons. After a couple of hours I had nineteen conversations but not one sale. Discouraged, I walked the two miles back to the office, convinced that I would never be a salesman.

I decided that there are people who can succeed on their own and those who depend on others. Obviously, I was lacking self-reliance. I recognized, fatalistically, that since I could not succeed in selling, I would always have to take jobs that would be less threatening and less rewarding. By the time I returned to the company I was thoroughly depressed.

Two weeks later, as I was clearing my desk of papers, I came across my notes of that discouraging morning. As I read the notes, I realized that of the nineteen people I had contacted, two had requested samples of my product. Walking home that evening through the wet snow, I asked myself, "Why hadn't I remembered those two positive responses?" Obviously I was so disillusioned by the seventeen negative responses that I had become emotionally numb to any positive reactions.

Appreciating Failure

I had been conditioned to believe that success was based on succeeding most of the time. Suddenly reality had changed, and I realized that *success is based on failing most of the time.* I needed to change my expectations, not of myself, but of others' receptivity to my efforts. New guidelines had to be formed. Failure was now a process that I needed to appreciate.

The next morning I delivered the samples and told my two prospects

I would call in a few days for their response. As I walked back to the company I wondered, "Why didn't I call on anyone else in the building, and why didn't I ask the two people to try my samples and make a decision immediately?" I realized I was avoiding any further rejection.

Expectations Create Determination

A few days later I returned and asked my prospects how they felt about the products. Encouragingly, one person bought carbon paper. In only a few hours of work I had a new account. I was inspired by the thought that I could do this once a day. I went back to my boss and told him I was ready to sell full time. He assigned the Wall Street territory to me. In the first nine days I opened ten new accounts. I had learned that expectations came in two parts: one was my expectation of myself, and the other was my expectation of reality.

Think of the expectations we have of ourselves. The more we expect of ourselves the greater our determination to excel. For those who need to achieve something significant, gain recognition and become financially independent, expectations motivate us to persevere until our needs are satisfied.

> The greater our expectations, the greater
> our determination to excel.

Next consider our expectations of other people. Maybe we are used to people accepting us and treating us pleasantly. How do we feel when reality does not meet our expectations and we have to fail most of the time to succeed? If we become discouraged we might decide that we expected too much of ourselves and, in disappointment, lower our expectations. While this might eliminate further disappointment, it will also compromise our self-esteem. We may have eliminated the emotional pain of failure and rejection but have sacrificed the satisfaction of achievement, recognition and financial independence.

As my success with Old Town continued, my confidence grew. I was ready to try IBM again. Knowing that IBM people tend to be intelligent and well educated convinced me to respond in the interview in a very serious manner. The manager was an emotional person. I was calm and relaxed as I described my success with Old Town. The manager dismissed me saying, "You lack emotions and excitement."

During this period of 1961 to 1962 I had begun my graduate degree in marketing management from the City University of New York. I was learning so much, so quickly that I soon felt encouraged to try again at IBM. This time I would impress the manager with my enthusiasm. I would express myself with energy.

This manager was a big man who sat there smoking a cigar. I leaned forward and, with excitement, told him that I believed in IBM products and why I would be a great salesman for his company. When I was finished he explained in a deep, resonant voice, "Young man, the reason why you are not qualified to sell for IBM is because you are too emotional."

I was becoming confused. Regardless of how enthusiastic or serious I was, I kept being rejected. Gradually, I realized that people are different. I criticized myself for having taken twenty-three years to learn such a simple lesson. The next time I would relate to the manager based on his style of personality. Within six months I felt the courage to try again.

In June of 1963, I made my fourth attempt. The IBM manager was an outgoing, pleasant man by the name of Hank Schick. I sensed that my aggressive, serious side would be inappropriate. I turned myself to that facet of my personality that was friendly and expressive. This time I easily established rapport and was finally hired.

Confronting Reality

Hank assigned me to the garment district of New York City. This territory was considered the most difficult in the country. The people in the garment industry live in a very competitive business environment. They struggle to survive on a small profit margin. Because of the stress, they are frequently hostile. Initially, I was pleased to be given this challenge. I wanted to prove to IBM that I could succeed in such a difficult environment.

On my first day on quota, I began walking into offices and giving my presentation. After being rejected, I would continue on to the next potential prospect. On the fifth call, I confronted more rejection than I had expected.

The receptionist was a young woman, probably just out of high school. She seemed pleasant and friendly. Enthusiastically, I introduced myself: "My name is Art Mortell, with IBM, and we have these fantastic new products that can revolutionize your entire operation. If I can show your boss a way to increase the production of his office by 50 percent would he give me fifteen minutes of his time?"

She smiled and said, "Get the %#*# out of here." I just stood there, speechless. She then pointed to the door, and, having no idea what to say, I left. I made a few more calls but kept confronting various forms of verbal abuse. My definition of the word *receptionist* was changing quickly. I was also losing confidence in myself. What was I doing wrong?

I realized that my problem was originating in my mind. I had been thinking to myself "I want people to like me, invite me into their office, be receptive to me and buy my machines." Yet this was not what I was experiencing. Reality was very different from my expectations. Again, I was becoming disappointed and frustrated.

> **Frustration is measured by the distance between our expectations and reality.**

Soon I found myself staying in the office each day. I would send out direct mail, hoping for a positive response. I would telephone the customers I inherited and tell them I was their new salesman and to call me if they needed me, but I was not making any cold calls or trying to schedule any appointments.

I knew that if I continued in this defensive pattern my manager would discover how ineffective I had become and fire me. I thought to myself, "I've worked too hard to quit so quickly. I've got to think of a solution. Now what *is* my problem?"

I decided my problem was my ego. I realized I was not sensitive, but oversensitive. Now what's the solution? The solution was to get rid of the problem. Since the problem was my lack of maturity, I decided that my solution also would be unadult, or childlike. I imagined that my territory with IBM was a make-believe room filled with prospects who had become imaginary objects. Each object was labeled "yes" or "no." My only job was to pick up each object, determine the label and separate those that said "no" from those labeled "yes."

Applying this philosophy to my real prospects, I discovered, on the average, that for every forty-three labeled negative, I found one labeled positive. This imaginary scenario disengaged my mind from all the negative feedback and focused my thoughts on those who were receptive to me. In ten months, before being transferred to California, I opened seventy new accounts, but *I didn't start succeeding until I learned how to fail.*

If our expectations of ourselves and others are unrealistic, we need to change them. Whenever we are frustrated we should ask ourselves two questions:

What is reality?

What are my expectations?

When we were children and we took a test most of us expected to answer most questions correctly. In the business arena we usually experience a far different ratio of failure to success. As the percentage of success changes, our expectations also need to change. We often need to fail frequently before we can expect to succeed. Rather than lowering our expectations we need to stay committed to our objectives while changing what we expect. By no longer expecting to always be accepted, we can more easily deal with difficult people.

Consider the origins of our expectations of ourselves. Some of us might have been told in childhood that seeking financial success can be very stressful. If we believed such thoughts, then we might have decided to expect less of ourselves and seek a less threatening position.

Others of us may have been ambitious. Maybe someone said, "I expect you to persevere until you succeed and become financially independent." The higher our expectations, the more we need to accomplish before we feel successful.

Apart from what we expect of ourselves are the expectations we formulate of the world around us. Some of us have been conditioned to believe that most people will love us. In my case, my mother loved me, regardless of the way I performed. Her unconditional love allowed me to feel secure. Unfortunately, school made me feel insecure. My teachers did not love me automatically, and I had to perform to be accepted.

Often negative feedback can be an emotional shock. What happens when we have ambitious objectives but we are emotionally unprepared for difficult times and negative feedback? When our preconceived ideas of the world around us are in direct contrast with reality then we will become frustrated. The greater the gap between where we are and where we need to be, the greater our frustration.

We then have a choice:

To lower our expectations by deciding we never should have tried and walk away from the challenge that is upsetting us

or

To change our expectations of the reality we are confronting so that the challenges no longer overwhelm us but strengthen our self-image.

We need to change our expectations of reality. *The old concept of failure is no longer valid.* Instead of protecting ourselves from failure we should *pursue and appreciate the wisdom* it offers us.

Strengthening Our Self-Image

Just as we need to understand the roots of our expectations, we also need to recognize the origins of our self-image. The more success and positive feedback we gain, the more positive our self-image most likely will become. Yet what is our self-image based on? If our feelings about ourselves are dependent upon success and acceptance, then what will happen to our self-image if success requires failing most of the time and being rejected? Failure and rejection might then damage, destroy or reduce our self-image. The way we rebound from such setbacks is by changing the way we develop self-acceptance. We need to find our strength and acceptance within ourselves.

> Our self-image needs to be based, not on the reactions of others, but on our own sense of value.

Becoming mature and successful depends on our self-image being based, not on winning or losing, nor being loved or rejected, but on our own sense of our value. Then, regardless of what happens, we will continue to grow more secure and confident. If our self-image rises and falls depending on whether we succeed or how people feel about us, then our emotions will be riding a continuous roller coaster. One moment we might be happy and elated. A moment later we might be tumbling into depression. We might become so exhausted by this roller coaster of emotions that we will want to get off. If that becomes our decision, we will soon find ourselves seeking secure situations. We may find ourselves on the sidelines, watching other people enjoying the adventures of life.

As our sense of identity becomes stronger, our self-esteem will increase. Soon we will be stimulated by defeat. As our personality strengthens, we will begin to capitalize on negative feedback. As our confidence level increases, we will start to thrive on stressful situations. As an example, when selling for IBM, I reminded myself of how many unreceptive people I would meet before finding someone who needed me. The thought that I could help someone insulated me from rejection.

Fine-Tuning Our Thoughts

The air is filled with radio waves, of the sounds of music, sports events and news reports. Yet, we cannot hear any of the voices or the music unless we first turn on a radio. At that point we may hear only static. We have to turn the dial and tune in. Even then we will most likely find stations we do not want. We have to keep turning the dial until we find what we enjoy, and then fine-tune the dial until the program we have selected sounds perfect.

Our minds are like radios. Each day we need to turn them on so that we can hear our thoughts. Then we have to turn the dial to determine our choices. Next we select the thoughts we prefer. If we consistently enjoy the way one selection makes us feel, we can program our minds so that we may stay tuned to that frequency of energy. Then, from that day on, we can always think and feel the way we want to, merely by hitting certain buttons. We program our minds to those thoughts that create the desired emotions and reactions. One way is by repeating thoughts that keep us in positive momentum.

> **We can program our minds to produce the desired reactions.**

Unfortunately, too many of us have been programmed by negative feedback. A critical parent or teacher may cause us to become critical of ourselves. We then have difficulty dealing with rejection. By readjusting our expectations to an ever-changing reality, we capitalize on the challenges that confront us. Only then will we eliminate frustration and think and feel in a way that keeps us in balance.

We can disengage from all our frustrations by taking twenty minutes to find a quiet place. The process can include exercise, meditation, or reading a book. Gradually, we will be able to clear our minds of the stress. Then we can develop new ideas and make more objective decisions. We can stay calm rather than backing off or lashing out and being hostile.

> **We program our minds to feel stimulated by our challenges.**

> **Expecting rejection can prepare us for the unpredictable.**

> **We begin to succeed when we learn how to fail.**

2
Reaching Crossroads

> Failure is a maturing process.

As we become older, we are able to deal more easily with stressful situations and become more mature or more inhibited. We need to recognize the choices we have when reaching the crossroads of life. For some of us, crossroads are traumatic places. We may have lost a loved one or gone bankrupt. For others of us, the disappointments may have been minor, but more frequent. Maybe the challenges have all been positive as we have moved from one accomplishment to the next. Why do we become more confident or more defensive at crossroads?

We have two paths from which to choose. One takes us on an adventurous journey. We feel exhilarated by the opportunity to reach new levels of success. We also might confront the possibility of disappointment. The other path is safe and familiar. This path of least resistance, though comfortable, also includes the danger of boredom.

Isaac Fleischman was a director of the U.S. Patent Office. He was fascinated by the fact that, during periods of economic depression, as unemployment increased, so did the issuing of patents. Once he spoke of his "perverse fondness for the dark days when the human spirit becomes ingenious." I have always been encouraged by that thought.

In 1992 millions of people were in a financial crisis. The unemployment rate in the United States was officially at 7 percent and, in actuality, around 11 percent. The difference was based on two million unemployed workers who were not counted in the statistics. These people were so discouraged by their unemployment benefits ending and the constant rejection of their job applications that they had stopped trying.

Why do some of us, when confronting difficult times, become discouraged, while others become more creative and determined? Maybe the answer is in our expectations; we demand so much of ourselves that we can never give up. When reality falls short of what we expected, we must renew our ingenious spirit. Our success begins with our ability to manage our expectations of ourselves and the reality we are experiencing.

Two children take the same test. One child receives a B and the other a C. Which child is happy and which one is disappointed? The child with the B is unhappy because this child expected an A, while the child with the C is pleased, having expected to get a D or to have failed.

> **Whether we experience failure or success is unimportant; what is important is the way we deal with the experience.**

Whether or not we capitalize on what happens begins with our expectations. When we expect to fail frequently before succeeding, then failure, rather than discouraging us, stimulates us to persevere and become innovative.

Imagine that you are starting a business. You have a list of one hundred companies that need your product. You make twelve telephone calls and do not experience a single positive response. Do you feel rejected and depressed? Do you find yourself reading the Wall Street Journal and telephoning friends to discuss this weekend's social gathering? Do you think of quitting?

You shouldn't. Do not expect success to come easily. Few people are born geniuses or succeed spontaneously. One of my favorite quotes is from Michelangelo, "If you knew how hard I worked you wouldn't consider me a genius."

> **Most of us will succeed only to the extent we are willing to suffer through many disappointments.**

Jump-Starting Your Brain

With high expectations of yourself and realistic expectations of the rest of the world, you may actually become stimulated by negative responses. You might even need twenty rejections in the morning to "jump-start your brain" and create an adrenal reaction.

Those who quit are either thinking too little of themselves or ignoring the lessons of reality. When they confront tough times, they often decide, "I guess I never should have tried in the first place." When these people reach crossroads, they take the safe path. They are disinclined to tackle the danger that is invariably within every adventure and opportunity. There is so much to learn from disappointing experiences. One lesson is in learning how our expectations influence the way we think during difficult times.

> **If we expect reality to be a continuous challenge, we will do better during the dark days.**

Every success I have ever experienced has prepared me for a more challenging opportunity. The difficulty of finishing college was simple compared to succeeding with Old Town. The challenge with IBM was even more difficult. Likewise teaching college was easy compared to starting my own business. Failure has become an old friend.

Many of us, while having high expectations, often take failure and rejection too personally. Though our determination forces us to persevere, our self-image may be tarnished by defeat and the unkindness of others. While we may achieve our objectives, in the process we too often may experience periods of prolonged anger or depression.

We must never allow adversity, negative feedback and stress to cause us to compromise our aspirations. Whenever we are disappointed we need to stay committed to our objectives while reevaluating what we expect of reality. By doing so, we will eventually discover how to enjoy all the experiences en route to reaching our goals.

In 1986, Don Vehlhaber reached a crossroads in his life. Now a senior manager in the management consulting department of the accounting firm KMPG, Peat Marwick, Don told me:

> It was the toughest period of my life. My company had a good product, and other companies wanted a piece of our pie. As the competition increased the pie got sliced so thin that we were on the verge of bankruptcy. Then my mother, father and grandmother died in quick succession. I felt I had been hit so often and so hard, especially being the executor of the estate and having to face the loss every day. Finally my wife confronted me, "You can sit here the rest of your life or do something about it." Action was the option I chose, and I've

been in control ever since. Regardless of how you feel, you have to be productive and go back to work.

Face adversity, reevaluate the problem and focus on the solution.

I don't believe in failure. Failure only occurs when you stop seeking solutions. Instead of accepting failure, you change your environment. You alter reality so you don't fail.

The road to success can be less stressful if we simply decide that *failure is only an experience that prompts us to try a different approach.* When we truly accept that idea then we create a different energy level. Rather than become depressed or angry from experiences that were disappointing, we become more determined.

Keeping a Sense of Humor

In 1948 Tom Dewey was the governor of New York and running for the presidency against Harry Truman. The polls had Dewey so far ahead of President Truman that on the evening of the elections, before the voting was completed, the Chicago Daily Tribune ran the headline "Dewey Defeats Truman."

On that same evening, as people were still voting, Tom asked his wife, while having dinner, "Darling, how is it going to feel to sleep with the president of the United States?" She said, "Personally, I'm looking forward to it."

The next morning over breakfast, as they read the newspaper reports of Truman's upset victory, she asked, "Tom, am I going to Washington or is Harry coming here?" Failure renews our humility. We cannot take ourselves too seriously. We need to keep our sense of humor.

When we reach crossroads we choose the adventurous path.

Strengthening our self-image helps us keep our sense of humor.

3

Learning
from
Failure

Anticipating that we might fail can prepare us for disappointment.

Jim King has been successful in marketing for Control Data and in management for Duquesne Systems. When Duquesne merged with another software firm, Jim's position was eliminated. Suddenly he was unemployed. He had reached a crossroad in his life that he had no desire to confront. He had to choose between seeking employment in a job market that seemed to be shrinking or going into business for himself.

Appreciating Adversity

Jim's ability to think through an emotionally disturbing problem is one of his major strengths. He shared his thoughts with me:

> You've got to understand that the greatest problem is often not the problem but the way the problem makes you feel. As you examine the problem you begin to realize you have a choice: you may react defensively or become energized by the challenge.
>
> When we experience a significant loss such as losing a good job

and significant income, we might also lose a major source of our identity. We may feel, deep within ourselves, an emptiness, as though we are in an emotional vacuum. If we allow this trauma to trigger a negative momentum, we will soon feel as though we are lost and immobilized by despair. The result is depression. The solution is to pull yourself out of these bad feelings. But how do you do this when you can't find the energy to get started? You begin by filling the emotional vacuum with some meaningful activity.

You cannot worry too much about whether you will fail or succeed. Otherwise you might become so concerned about immediate results that you feel overwhelmed. You need to focus on doing something productive. In other words, you tackle any activity that makes you feel you are worthwhile.

As I listened to Jim I thought of the activities that can strengthen our self-image and increase our confidence to persevere:

- Write a plan of action and don't procrastinate—do it.

- Consider what steps we can take each day that will bring us closer to our target.

- Tap into our unused resources by taking on a new challenge.

- Appreciate what we are already doing correctly and polish our most promising skills.

- Evaluate successful people and adopt their attributes.

Jim continued:

I know that one of my primary strengths in business is my ability to make difficult decisions. When I sold computers for Control Data, and was number one in performance, I had to decide when to ask the prospect for a decision. If I asked too soon I might antagonize the buyer, and if I waited too long I might lose him to a competitor. When I was in management my results were usually a by-product of making difficult decisions quickly.

Now I had to *manage myself* by making some difficult decisions. I knew the first part of the decision-making process was understanding the problem. While the problem was that I had lost something important to me, I decided that maybe I really had found something even more important. I had found my freedom.

The Value of Being Lost

Jim's thoughts reminded me of a time when I was driving on vacation in Europe and got lost. I felt a sense of panic. My family was depending on me, and I did not know where I was. Then I decided that I was not lost, but rather was exploring a place I had never been before. The anxiety subsided into feelings of exhilaration. I was driving down cobblestone streets through medieval villages and visiting old churches. Asking for directions in a different language was very difficult, but I no longer cared. This undiscovered country, which had frightened me, was now energizing. I was learning the value of being lost. If we change the way we think, then losing anything, such as our job, can free us to drive the back roads of our life and explore new opportunities. Jim told me:

> For the first time in my career I was free. Yet freedom can excite you or frighten you. I had to make a decision to capture the opportunities. If I struggled to find another corporate job, I would always wonder what I might have accomplished and who I might have become. Gradually, I realized that I had no choice. The decision was obvious. As Roosevelt said, "The only thing we have to fear is fear itself." What had been frightening before was now motivating me to capitalize, not on the problem, but the challenge to explore a new world.

Losing something of value does not have to be a disappointing experience. We can decide to seize the opportunity to go beyond the boundaries of our predictable life. Jim understands that there is an experience more upsetting than failure and that is the *fear of failing*.

Jim's story recently took another positive turn. As a management consultant and trainer, Jim worked with companies of different sizes. When he conducted a management strategy seminar in 1991, the chief executive officers (CEOs) of several local Pittsburgh companies attended. A year later, when one of the CEOs needed a senior sales executive, he offered Jim the job. Jim is now in charge of sales for a leading high-tech company, Vortex Systems. By forging ahead confidently in the face of uncertainty, Jim now has the skills to be successful inside the corporate world or on his own. He can do either as new circumstances unfold.

Apprehension and Confidence

I can remember, as a child, playing with a ball along the ocean's edge. The ball began to float away. As I waded into the water, I became apprehensive, went back to the shore and lost the ball. Later in the day, as I became more confident, I enjoyed walking deeper into the water until it reached my face. My mother then explained, "If you were as confident earlier as you are now, you would have easily gotten your ball back."

Worrying too much about making mistakes can cause us to stop trying. However, if we make the effort and fail, we might say, "That wasn't so bad, I think I'll try again." Confronting negative resistance positions us to more aggressively pursue our goal. If we succeed, the reward is a new strength to our self-image. This enhances our level of confidence so we feel comfortable taking on new responsibilities.

Extending Ourselves

Recently, I gave a lecture for Sun Data in Atlanta and met Susan Greene. After twenty years of being a homemaker, mother and frequent volunteer, Susan entered the doctoral program in human resources at Georgia State University. She then joined Sun Data, a computer company. Susan told me what she was conditioned to believe as a child:

> You must always follow the rules. Unfortunately, there was no place for errors, and I found myself always afraid of failure. I never strayed from the perimeters. The result was that I kept accepting my life as it was, even when I felt miserable. The fear of risking or taking a chance prevented me from ever going beyond the boundaries of my life.
>
> I only began to move toward happiness when I began to counsel myself through my own mental limitations. I would deal with each negative event, determine how I felt about it and look for the good in it until the circumstance was converted into a positive item. Then I would go on to my next challenge. I looked to the future rather than dwelling upon the past. I've learned that failure is essential. You take chances and when you make a mistake you forgive yourself.

We forgive ourselves when we are not perfect.

> You are not really living unless you are failing at least 30 percent of the time. You need to step out and go beyond where you have been before. Once I read Joseph Conrad's book *Lord Jim* in which Lord Jim goes to war believing he will be a hero, only to discover in battle that he is a coward. I learned this is often what happens to people who have high ideals. They become perfectionists. When they fail they feel ashamed and give up. If we aren't measuring up to our own expectations, we too often drop out. We each need to keep our high expectations but learn to forgive ourselves when we are not perfect.
>
> I find that every day I have failures and successes. I still tend to brood about things that go wrong, but by trying to see in each case

what I learned, what was positive about the experience, I find that my life is much richer and rewarding.

Making the necessary adjustments gives us positive momentum.

We all tend to pursue those challenges in which we feel secure, comfortable and confident. Yet there is always the next level, such as the next position in management or starting our own business. When we recognize the opportunity, though we may feel insecure, we can still initiate the process. First, we evaluate how we will enter this new arena. Second, we imagine all the paths that can get us to our destination. Then we have the courage to confront our thoughts of failing. Otherwise, if we allow our fears to get in our way, we might never even get started.

Our problem is often not with the actual failure but the anticipation of defeat. Just the thought of "wiping out" can immobilize us. Too often we negatively believe that it is *better not to try and to hope that if we had we would have succeeded than to try and fail and find there was no hope.* The fear of failure can make cowards of us all. We avoid new challenges rather than develop our potential. The solution is to develop the *courage to fail.*

Attacking Our Fears

Joyce Poulson was trained to be an occupational therapist. Instead she entered business by joining the Service Bureau Company. Then the division went out of business, and Joyce was out of a job. She described her approach to the problem:

> This was the first real job I ever had. Life had been easy for me, and I took my success for granted. When I suddenly found myself out of work, I was paralyzed by fear. I was staying home and wasn't making the effort to find employment. Then I decided I had nothing to lose. I have to admit that *without adversity there is no growth.* Once I decided "What's the big deal?" I began trying and soon was making better than three times what I had made before. I will never be out of a job again because I now understand that there are always opportunities for those who attack their fears.
>
> There was a time in my life when I seemed to be confronting one crossroad after another. When I took the more adventurous path, I increased my opportunities as well as the chance of being disap-

pointed. These crossroads can become a way of life for us as we are driven by the energy of the challenges.

Positive and Negative Fears

On New Year's Eve of 1964 I left New York City and moved to California. While still selling for IBM, I began teaching at Pasadena College in the evenings.

In 1966 I took a sales training class. The ideas presented in the seminar had value but were out of date. The program was based on concepts from the 1930s. They reminded me of a Model T Ford. It will get you where you want to go, but there are so many more efficient ways to make the trip. I thought, "If these people are doing so well financially, in spite of teaching such old concepts, then I should start my own training program."

At the same time, I was worried. I had a mortgage to pay, and my fourth child would soon be born. I needed the security of IBM and Pasadena College. Gradually, I realized that the fear of failing was preventing me from trying.

Then a question entered into my mind: "How would I feel if I never tried?" I knew the answer. More than having regrets, I would resent myself for the rest of my life. I could imagine myself as an old man, thinking, "What might I have accomplished if I had made the effort?" We all know people who have disregarded opportunities only to wish later, "If only I had tried."

> **We resolve resentment by conquering our fears.**

I knew that my life was on the verge of a major crisis. If I left IBM, I might lose my emotional and financial security. If I didn't try, I would fail myself by not discovering what I could accomplish on my own. The conflict was very stressful. Somehow I would have to deal with these immobilizing fears.

I began to understand that I actually had two kinds of fears. In simple terminology, I could label them as positive or negative fears. The positive fears were warning me of possible danger, and the negative fears were preventing me from succeeding. Our positive fears prepare us for the unexpected. Awareness of what might go wrong enhances the possibility of success.

Too often our optimism causes us to lose objectivity. We need to be critical of ourselves in a constructive way. Without being objective we might be so optimistic as to convince ourselves that we will succeed regardless of what might happen. This assumption creates the illusion that we are incapable of error. Instead, we want to step outside ourselves so we can see ourselves as others do. Then we can make recommendations as though we were speaking to someone else.

> **Evolve beyond the positive or negative and be creatively critical.**

Think of how easily we can be objective for the benefit of others. We can see their problems and develop significant solutions. Unfortunately, we often have difficulty guiding ourselves through the entanglements of our journey. Our ego gets in the way, costing us the benefit of our own objectivity. We need to be as critical of ourselves as we are of others. This requires detaching from our ego and seeing ourselves as though in a mirror.

If we listen to our fears, we might quickly identify whether or not they are for our benefit. The negative fears frighten us until we have given up on our goals, and our enthusiasm to persevere is neutralized. We can hear them saying, "Why bother? It isn't worth the effort. Remember what happened last time. You might hurt yourself. You will only fail and make a fool of yourself."

Forecast the Storm

> **Being ready for the unexpected increases our chances of succeeding.**

The positive fears prepare us for the unpredictable. They increase our chances of reaching our expectations by anticipating possible pitfalls. Even more important, we ascertain the reasons why we might fail. To those who question the value of such negative thinking, consider the purpose of checking the weather forecast before taking a vacation. There is value in predicting the conditions before embarking on a new journey. We don't want to find ourselves in the middle of a storm wondering, "How did I get myself in such a predicament?"

Equally, whether starting our own business, beginning a new career or acquiring greater responsibility, we need to forecast the problems before they occur. Otherwise, we might panic when surprised by possible disaster. Rather than being demoralized by the complexity of our challenge, we can experiment with the various choices. Then we can focus on those alternatives that offer the greatest likelihood of success.

> **The thought of adversity prepares us for the challenge.**

Many years ago I read a newspaper article about a man skydiving. He pulled the cord, the chute did not open and, in panic, he never pulled the emergency cord. The article discussed how this happens with some frequency. Many people, when they panic cannot function properly.

More recently, I read another article about a man skydiving. He pulled the cord, and his chute did not open. He pulled the emergency cord, and that did not open. Terrified but still able to reason, he thought quickly about his options. He realized that his only chance for survival was to land in a way that caused the least impact to his body. He leaned forward, landed on the front of his feet and went into an acrobatic tumble. Both ankles broke immediately. Though the rest of his body experienced abrasions and bruises, he broke no other bones. The man who could have lived died, and the man who would have died lived.

Our first challenge is dealing, not with failure, but with the thought of failing. We do not want our fears to cause us to panic nor our apprehensions to paralyze us. Instead, we want the thought of adversity to prepare us for the challenge. Then our fears can save us from disaster and misfortune.

In review, if our fears help us to prepare for any possible danger then they are positive. If their only effect is to prevent us from going beyond our present position, then they are negative. We need to defuse such fears, or they might immobilize us.

Incremental Steps to Success

One secret for success is to break our fears into such small segments that they lose their negative influence over us. We never want to take a step so great that if we fall we crash. The steps we take should be incremental so that if we fail, we do not fall but only stumble.

I loved the movie *What About Bob*. Bill Murray plays the role of a man who is overwhelmed by his fears. He is afraid of breathing because of germs. He is claustrophobic and will not ride in an elevator. He has to walk up forty flights of stairs to visit his psychiatrist, played by Richard Dreyfuss.

The psychiatrist has just had a new book published entitled *Baby Steps*. He advises Bill to break down his challenges into easy steps. Rather than worry about the formidable task that he wishes to accomplish, he should focus on one step at a time. We, too, should remember the ancient Chinese proverb that *"a journey of a thousand miles must begin with a single step."* Break down the challenges into stepping-stones. Then our failures will guide us along the adventurous path.

In 1966, when I was twenty-seven, the idea of baby steps meant starting my business on a part-time basis. While still selling for IBM and teaching college in the evening, I would begin lecturing one night per week. If I succeeded in reaching the first step, I would then take the next. Twenty-five years later I am rated as one of the top business lecturers in the United States, but I still think each day of how I can take my success one step further.

Continuous Movement

> Our positive momentum soon creates the desired results.

We need to place primary importance on continuous movement. Our consistency is crucial. If we take on too much, we may feel overwhelmed and want to quit. If we take on too little, we will be performing beneath our ability. We need to find a level of effort that stretches us without exhausting us. If we confront a problem, we can always reduce the difficulty a notch while still persevering. If we are doing better than we expected, we can accelerate our activity. This allows us the freedom to take on new responsibilities. Through this process, we form a productive routine. These successful habits prevent procrastination and complacency. Rather than thinking of what to do and working at succeeding, our energy flows effortlessly.

Imagining Our Performance

I would give my first lecture on September 14, 1967. Succeeding was very important to me. Yet, the more exhilarated I felt by the idea of performing well, the more apprehensive I felt that I might fail. I needed a way to feel confident, even though I had yet to succeed.

Of course, I had the positive experiences of selling for IBM and teaching college. But this presentation was new and different. Even more of a concern was the audience. I would be speaking to three times as many people as I had ever spoken to before, and most were my friends and neighbors. The more people I knew, the more concerned I was about the impression I would make and how they would feel about me. The solution was to create the confidence that would assure an effective performance.

A classic way of developing confidence before making the effort is to create the experience in one's imagination. If we can imagine ourselves performing successfully, we can generate the same confidence we would feel if we had actually achieved the goal. If we cannot imagine ourselves attaining the objective, then we will probably have difficulty even making an effort.

Every night, after dinner, I would walk the empty streets and imagine they were filled with people. Though dark I imagined that the lights were bright and in my mind I would begin my speech. I also imagined that I was someone else, sitting in the audience listening to myself. I found myself critical of nearly every sentence that was spoken. I would stop myself to discuss the necessary corrections. As the sentence improved, my objective voice would allow my ego to continue. I rehearsed the lecture, interweaving the corrections, until I knew I was ready.

That night, as I was introduced, my heart was pounding so loudly that I was sure the audience would realize how nervous I was. At the same time, I had the strange sense of confidence that they would enjoy what I would say. I had already imagined the audience in those empty streets being responsive to me. Afterwards, as people were congratulating me, I knew that what I had imagined had enabled me to succeed.

> **Creating the experience in our mind allows us to develop confidence in our self-image.**

Just as, succumbing to our fears, we can imagine we will fail, so, too, we can imagine ourselves succeeding. We can use our imagination to create any emotions that we wish.

Under hypnosis, we can be told that we are in a wonderful situation and immediately we will feel happy. Then, while still receptive to the hypnotist's suggestions, we can be told that our loved ones have died and our body is in pain. In that moment our elation will turn to despair. Correspondingly, we can imagine our life to be any way we wish. By doing so, we create emotions that cause us to feel good even though we are going through difficult times.

So often we imagine the world as we are afraid it might be. Then our imagined fears cause us to become defensive, and we fail. We might even doubt our success. Whatever success we experience may be forgotten as we dwell on our failures.

Such thoughts create feelings of apprehension. Our fears cause us to fail, which fulfills our negative prophecy. Instead we want to create confidence by *visualizing ourselves performing at our optimum level.*

To summarize, we all need to forecast problems before they occur. One way to conquer problems is to break them down into small bits. Then we can imagine ourselves succeeding in small increments before we try. When we create a positive experience in our mind, we enhance our self-image. In this way the apprehension subsides, and our confidence is increased.

Imagine the weather is hot and the pool of water looks very inviting. What if we dip our toes in the water and it is cold? Now the thought of jumping into the water chills us. If we were to plunge into the water, it might be as cold as we anticipated, but as we begin swimming we get acclimated to the temperature. Soon we are refreshed and glad that we jumped in.

Life is the same way. If we anticipate the experience, we may be chilled by the apprehension of defeat and the thought of making a fool of ourselves. If we throw ourselves into the situation, the difficulty might be at least as great as we were afraid it would be. However, if we keep moving we will soon be enjoying the challenge. The end result might even be one of triumph as well as the recognition that the adventure was worthwhile.

When we were children, we didn't run until we first learned to walk. We took baby steps. When we fell, we had not failed. Though we landed on our rear, we laughed and tried again. The applause of our family, merely because we were trying, was a constant encouragement.

We need to be children again, evolving by learning and growing from our mistakes. What we discover then propels us into the future.

> **Our interpretation defines the event.**

We all experience times when we feel disappointed and depressed. We might even believe that we will always be unhappy. Dr. Karl Gretz conducts seminars to help people through their dark days. He made these observations:

> Sometimes we need to close our eyes and make a list of our best memories. We need to relive happy memories to lighten our mood. Remembering our past successes can create the energy that replaces feelings of discouragement.
>
> Successful people remember themselves in positive experiences. Discouraged people remember unhappy memories. Yet, each of us can change the focus of our memories, which will then change our feelings about ourselves. If you are remembering the bad experiences, you might feel like a loser. Whether you are dealing with a remembered experience or a current experience, it is not the event but the interpretation of the event that determines how you feel.

Finding Purpose

Karl rephrases the ideas of Viktor Frankl from his classic book *Man's Search for Meaning:* "If life has meaning, then all pain and suffering is meaningful and bearable. If life has no purpose, then the smallest suffering can be devastating."

When we discover our purpose in life and interpret our experiences as meaningful we create a positive force of energy. If we feel no sense of purpose we will have difficulty dealing with even minor frustrations.

There are two criteria that determine whether or not the challenge is appropriate in business. First is the opportunity for financial success. The other is ego satisfaction. We want both at the same time.

If our challenges are meaningful, but our interpretation of our experiences creates negative memories, then we will think less of ourselves and feel badly. We want all the factors for success working for our benefit.

Wizards and Warriors

Steve Drozdeck, who is the author of many business books including *What They Don't Teach You In Sales 101,* was once a stockbroker for Merrill Lynch. Steve believes we all have the potential to be a wizard and a warrior. Wizards are mature, brilliant and can see reality as they wish it to be. Warriors have the ability to do battle with reality until they have fulfilled their purpose. Steve enjoys developing the duality of his personality. The philosophy of his wizard and the strength of his warrior help him to make the necessary changes. Steve's success begins with using failure as a way of increasing his chances of succeeding. He writes:

> Failure is a pure manifestation of the mind. If you know you are going to eventually look back on the disappointment and laugh about it, then why wait. If you also know that you eventually will deal with the disturbance, then why not deal with it now. The anticipated failure is usually worse than the actual event.

Directing our thoughts helps us capitalize on failure, and acting helps us deal with rejection.

Steve does not believe in rejection. He believes only in the opportunities that challenge us to master the circumstances. He reminds us that the way to deal with rejection is to make it a game. We enjoy our challenges and, no matter what happens, have a good time. We get from our lives what we ask if we are willing to do battle with failure, rejection and stress. For this reason Steve keeps a few poetic words in his mind:

> I bargained with life for a penny
> and life would pay me no more
> no matter how much I cried in the evening
> when I counted my scanty store
>
> for life is a just employer
> he gives you what you ask
> and once you have set the wages
> only you must bear the task
>
> I worked for a menial hire
> only to learn dismayed
> that any wages I had asked of life
> life would have willingly paid.

Imagining ourselves succeeding creates confidence.

Failing teaches us how to maneuver through our obstacles.

When our life is filled with purpose, then stress has value.

4
Fulfilling
Our Dreams

Successful people view risk from a different perspective.

As a child I read the imaginative stories of Jules Verne, the nineteenth-century French novelist. I was fascinated with his science fiction stories of submarines diving 20,000 leagues under the sea and people landing on the moon.

In the early 1950s we were told that, by the year 2000, we might reach the moon. Then the Russians launched Sputnik. The Russian victory became a U.S. humiliation, but this disappointment motivated the United States to accelerate space exploration. New expectations intensified the determination to win. A race to the moon had begun. Early U.S. efforts were frustrated by spectacular defeat, as rockets misfired and exploded. Still, within a short time, the United States won the race, and landing on the moon became a reality.

Cervantes's character Don Quixote wished that dreams and reality were the same. At Cape Canaveral the dreams of Jules Verne became reality. Unfortunately, many of us are not willing to experience the failure and humiliation that are often required when *converting dreams into reality.*

Tragic Times and Winning

Listening to others who have lived through tragedy can help us make difficult decisions and eventually win. Mark Klein was planning on attending college after he completed his three years with the Marines. In 1958 he came home on leave. His father was awaiting Mark's return for a tragic reason. He wanted Mark to take care of the family when he committed suicide. It was Mark who found his father in the garage and cut him down.

> I felt I was in a Shakespearian tragedy. It was as though the fates had turned against me. My dreams had died along with my dad. This was my first major hurdle in life and my first real feeling of panic. When I left the Marines, rather than go to college, I went to work in a gas station. Still, I felt a strong conviction to do better.
>
> Nine months later I was fortunate to be hired by IBM as a draftsman. After doing well in that job, I requested an opportunity in sales. Once I was promoted into this position, a degree was no longer crucial. Making quota was all that was important, and I excelled. When I became a manager in Atlanta, with hundreds of people reporting to me, I had exceeded my own expectations.
>
> In 1978 we discovered that my son had cancer. Shortly thereafter, I watched as my house and twenty years of belongings burned to the ground. Then in 1979 IBM asked me to transfer from Atlanta. I didn't want to move, so I decided to look for a new job.
>
> I received a job offer with a small software company. This was my opportunity to become a big fish in a small bowl. I was infatuated with promises, including the possibility of becoming president. I was unfamiliar with the uniqueness of the business and lost the job. For the first time I found myself out of work.
>
> I had never failed before. Suddenly, I was losing this wonderful life-style that I had worked so hard to acquire. I was filled with anxiety and tremendous tension. Within one year's time my son had cancer, my home was destroyed and I was unemployed.
>
> Then, in April of 1980 I joined Memorex. I understood the business, and I succeeded. My son's cancer was in remission, and we were living in California. I no longer had any problems, and the years passed. In 1987 my company was purchased by Europeans who decided to change management, and I was terminated. In 1989 my son's cancer reoccurred for the third time, and we lost him in March of 1990.
>
> With my back against the wall, I became a consultant. This is what people do when they are out of work. In late 1990 I arranged to buy Computer Media Technology. At the age of fifty-four I am starting again. Rather than working for a corporation I now own my own business. After thirty years I have fulfilled a dream of being an entrepreneur. My small company sells computer supplies and accessories, which is what I sold at IBM. I am returning to my strengths.

> **Develop a strategy for persevering through tragedy.**

Progressing requires focusing on a challenge you understand. You increase your chances of succeeding by utilizing your strengths. For example, I am able to relate to most anyone. When in turmoil I can feel comfortable depending on people. Friendships can provide advice and information that can increase the possibility of making sensible decisions. They also create a sense of support that can keep your spirits up during the bad times.

   I am a competitor, though hopefully not to a fault. The Marine Corps and IBM molded my beliefs. I refuse to lose. I am not a quitter. On my office wall I have the words of Vince Lombardi:

> Winning is not a sometimes thing
> it is an all time thing
> you don't win once in awhile,
> you don't do things right once in awhile,
> you do things right all the time
> there is no room for second place
> there is only one place
> and that's first place

Often people say to me, "How devastating it must have been for you, particularly the loss of your son." But I know that most everyone has experienced the death of a loved one or the loss of a job. We cannot dwell on the bad. If you want to live, you don't feel sorry for yourself. You don't look back. Your life is always unfolding into new frontiers right before your eyes.

   Identifying with Mark can help us to get through the bad times. Each of us must formulate our own philosophy for success. Then we decide which abilities we need to acquire if we are to accomplish what we have set before us.

> **We imagine the world as we wish it to be.**

> **We convert our dreams into reality.**

5
Capitalize on Adversity

> **Our ability to succeed is based on our willingness to experience failure.**

While teaching persuasion and management skills at Pasadena College, I began to question whether such subjects were really key factors for success. I was troubled by the fact that some students would use the ideas offered in class enthusiastically, while others seemed inhibited. Then I realized that the same situation existed within IBM. In a sales training class there were those who were receptive to trying new techniques and those who were apprehensive. I began thinking of those qualities successful people have that are missing in others.

Many people believe that enthusiasm is a primary factor for success. However, we need to question why some people try a new approach enthusiastically but then, if they don't get immediate results, stop trying. Others begin cautiously and, regardless of difficulty, build momentum until they achieve their objectives.

Wondering what causes success reminds me of Kim Fellwock who began selling in 1976 without any sales or business experience. In his first six months he set a record. As he put it to me:

No one had ever sold as little as I did and still stayed employed. I seemed to always feel bad about myself and constantly found reasons to procrastinate. It was tough to get out of bed. I had no idea what to do. My degree was in teaching, but I no longer cared to teach. I decided to learn how to succeed by taking seminars and reading books. I learned new strategies and techniques and began to improve. But compared to my associates, I was doing poorly, and my ego was being bruised by the struggle.

Years later I listened to Kim, now a vice president of training and sales development at Baxter Healthcare Corporation, introduce me as a speaker for his account executive conference:

> The more I understood how to sell, the more I realized that I did not understand myself. I was learning that success in business is a game that you play in your mind. I kept asking myself why some people succeed and others fail, and I never found the answer until I read a book in 1976 entitled *Anatomy of a Successful Salesman* by our speaker, Art Mortell. On page thirteen he says that the secret of success is simply "the ability to fail." He went on to explain that "most people are so afraid of failure and rejection that they spend their entire lives looking for comfortable situations where there are no risks or decisions to make and where they cannot possibly fail and be rejected. Your ability to fail and continue trying will determine your success. Without this ability all your goals will turn into empty dreams, your desire will be bottled up by fear, your confidence will be eroded by the first rejections, and all your knowledge and skills will be wasted for fear of failure."

After my lecture Kim and I spoke of what he referred to as mastering the inner game of failure and rejection:

> I grew up in an environment that was always easy for me. My parents were very positive, and I did better than average in school. When I went into business I experienced an emotional shock. People did not always like me. I was not used to rejection. I began to question my worth. I could feel my stomach turning, and I was not sleeping well. Once I began to view failure as a way of trying new ideas, I felt better.

Developing a New Philosophy

Why worry about your problems when, a year from now, they probably will not exist? The anxiety is soon gone when you convince yourself that, in the future, what is presently upsetting you will be a forgotten memory. The challenge is to laugh at your setbacks as a way of short-circuiting the frustration.

Sustaining Enthusiasm

> If we cannot accept failure, we will quickly lose our enthusiasm.

In 1974, IBM was in a period of consolidation and began training senior people for selling. Though they were mature and sophisticated, IBM was still emphasizing enthusiasm in the training and including humorous skits and songs.

I began my presentation by asking, "What's the highest paid profession?" They all yelled enthusiastically, "Sales." I said, "No, doctors," and the audience became very quiet.

I asked, "What's the second highest paid profession?" Half the audience cautiously said, "Sales?" I said, "No, executives."

Then I asked, "What's the third highest paid profession?" and one person said, "Plumbers."

Professional salespeople have been ranked as the third highest in income, behind doctors and executives. These professionals had the right answer, though not on the first try. Their response would not be correct until the third question, but they would not try three times in a row. If I was able to drown their enthusiasm within twenty seconds, then what would happen to any one of them when, alone, they experienced disappointment? The enthusiasm we bring to our job each day is of little value if we cannot deal with adversity.

Failure as an Illusion

If any one of us were homeless, we might be very happy to be given a one-room apartment and bus fare to work. On the other end of the financial success spectrum, if we were worth $10 million, and suddenly lost half, how would we feel? Most of us would be very upset to lose $5 million. One person is happy with bus fare, and the other is depressed with $5 million.

> One person's success can be someone else's disappointment.

My longtime friend George Seldin has been a successful entrepreneur for over twenty years. One of his favorite stories about how he first started his own company begins with the day he came to work and no one else showed up.

George was the sales manager for a struggling computer time-sharing company in Los Angeles. For several months the company owners had been trying desperately to raise capital to pay the bills and keep the company going. One day in early December of 1970 they just gave up.

> I came to work that beautiful California winter day, only to find that none of the owners were there. At first I thought they were at one of the many fund-raising meetings that seemed to evolve each day. However, at about eleven that morning I was still the only one in the office.
>
> I called the president's home and spoke with him. He told me it was all over—they could not raise another dime. I hung up the phone, took a deep breath and quickly sized up my options. I could go home and break the bad news to my wife, I could go out and have a drink or I could make some phone calls and see what was going on with the rest of my business contacts.
>
> I chose to get on the phone and call a good friend whom I had been dealing with. He told me about an opportunity to buy some used computer equipment his company was selling. Since I was familiar with the equipment I called several other companies that I thought might need these machines. I don't remember how many calls I made that first day, but by the end of the day I sold one of the machines. By the end of the week I sold several more and made more money than I had made in the last ten weeks.

Seven years later George was making ten times the salary he was making working for someone else, and a few years after that he was a multi-millionaire with several companies and over one hundred employees.

> I could have easily given up that day and taken pity on myself. I now realize how scared I really was and how I just had to do something to keep going. Today I won't allow myself to think of losing even though I lose many more deals than I ever make. I consider each situation a new opportunity, winning some and losing others but never giving up.

George also believes that going into business merely to make money is not only shortsighted but will eventually lead to failure:

> You need to be excited about your purpose, and you must build a company with a good staff and a real competitive edge such as quality and uniqueness. If money is your only motivator, you will be-

come simply an opportunist, but if you build a real company around good people, the money will come.

I asked George if he could recall any bad days that were especially distasteful. He told me about the day he had to fire the entire staff of one of his companies:

> I had started a newsletter for one of my companies that quickly turned into a full-fledged publishing company. We enjoyed tremendous success at first and became a leader in our niche.
>
> After several years some of the leading publishers wanted to buy our company. I was not willing to sell, as I always thought the price too low. After several years these companies forced us out of our position as leader in our field and eventually out of business. I suddenly found myself in the position of having to release the entire staff of my publishing company. It was not my only bad day, but I remember it as my worst. I called everyone together and gave them the news. We were a great team and a family. We all cried a little at that meeting, and I took the entire blame. I did not run out, and every person was paid their entire salary. Although we were not able to continue as a business, I had structured the company as a real entity and was able to sell the remaining assets for something in excess of $1 million.

Our reactions to failure and success originate in our perceptions.

George Seldin believed he failed as a publisher even though he made a million dollars at it. Whenever we become discouraged by defeat, we need to shape reality as we would shape a dream, take our failures and cast them into a different mold and convert them into what we wish them to be. Look at each failed attempt as a catalyst that stimulates us to pursue our objectives. *Gradually our dreams will materialize.*

Being Amused by Our Frailties

There are many ways to change our perceptions of reality. One is to find the humor in those situations that might otherwise upset us. Then we can more easily be risk-oriented. Whenever we feel reluctant to even try, we should remember John Glenn.

It was February 20, 1962, and John was walking to the rocket ship when a reporter asked him, "John, when you get up into orbit, what's going to happen if your rockets don't fire and you can't get back down?" He turned and said, "It's going to spoil my day."

John Glenn's short flight into space instantly transformed him into a national hero. The Senate was intrigued with the first flights of the astronauts, so after John landed he was invited to Washington. One senator asked him, "What were you thinking about as you were coming back through reentry?" John replied, "I was thinking to myself, as I was returning through space, that this capsule was manufactured by the lowest bidder."

Emptiness and Purpose

There are two forces in our lives. One is purpose, and the other is emptiness. Purpose fills our lives with meaning. The greater our sense of purpose, the more we enjoy the challenges of each day.

We also need to understand the concept of emptiness. In Michael Ende's classic novel and movie *The Neverending Story*, the young hero visits a kingdom that is disappearing. He discovers that this beautiful place is being taken over by nothingness, which occurs when people cease to dream. Without a sense of purpose our lives will have no meaning.

We are constantly in a battle between these two forces. When we stop dreaming, we lose our sense of purpose. Our lives are filled with emptiness. We want to remember Jules Verne, Don Quixote, and John Glenn.

> **We need to find the humor in our vulnerabilities.**

> **We need to be visionary.**

6
Explore
the
Unknown

> Unless we thrive on failure and rejection, we will
> become disheartened by defeat.

Taking Courage

In the third century B.C., Eratosthenes determined, at high noon in the city of Syene, that a stick of wood, perfectly vertical, cast no shadow. He also discovered that 500 miles away, at the exact same moment, a stick perfectly vertical cast a shadow of 7 degrees. The obvious reason: The earth was round.

Since 7 degrees is approximately 1/50 of 360 degrees, if every 7 degrees is 500 miles, then the full circle would be 25,000 miles. When the exact calculations were completed, Eratosthenes had determined the earth's circumference to within a few miles.

Eighteen hundred years later Christopher Columbus appealed to Spain for ships, men and supplies to travel beyond the horizon across an uncharted ocean to the Orient. The decision of whether or not to support him was left to scholars. These men explained that Columbus was reading the wrong maps. He thought the world was only 18,000 miles around. His figure was incorrect by 7,000 miles. The voyage to India, rather than being a few weeks, would take almost a year, and the tiny ships could not carry supplies for more than a couple of months.

Then, in January of 1492, the King and Queen of Spain, in celebration of having gained their independence from the Moors, granted Columbus his wish, by giving him three small ships. In October of that same year, Columbus landed on what he believed were islands off the coast of India. Three times he returned in an effort to find the mainland of India and the Orient. Today, rather than celebrate the accomplishment of Eratosthenes, who measured the earth accurately, we acknowledge Columbus who made four trips to the New World and died in 1506, never knowing where he had been.

> **Our willingness to extend beyond our boundaries frees us to explore the unknown.**

Discard the thought that "knowledge is power." Although Eratosthenes was highly accurate in his calculations, nothing resulted from his work. One of the secrets of success is our willingness, though ignorant of what is beyond the horizon, to explore the uncharted course. Our desire to extend ourselves frees us of our fears so that we can apply what we already understand. Even more important, we learn through discovery. Confronting risk can bring us to a new world that we would otherwise have never known existed.

> **Challenging ourselves is often the only way we acquire real knowledge.**

Enjoying the Adventure

Dan Mullane, a training manager for Advest, understands that only applied knowledge is power:

> In the adventure of business our challenge is to understand that the unpredictable is expected. The solution is to be flexible and enjoy the adventure rather than taking ourselves too seriously and becoming fearful. We learn to focus our efforts during difficult times. First, we do the best we can regarding the immediate challenge; second, we concentrate our energy into those opportunities on the horizon.

I've also learned to accept who I am. When I am honest with myself regarding my fears, I am able to trust myself to take risk. I then believe I can accomplish whatever I wish. I can now conceptualize my fears and the role they play in my life rather than taking them personally. We all need to recognize our fears and keep them in their proper place.

Allowing the essence of who we are to come through gives us a tremendous advantage. We need to develop our own way of accomplishing this advantage. The first step is self-exploration and reflection. The second is to focus on what is important. Every day I give it my best. I no longer have a fear of failure, particularly when I remember that our predicaments are only temporary.

Changing Our Thinking

There are only two ways in which we can fail: One is by *not trying* and the other is by *quitting*. Otherwise, we cannot fail. Possibly the experience was less than what we expected, but we must always ask ourselves, "What did I do right that allowed me to last as long as I did? Why, as an example, did my company hire me?"

Understand how Thomas Edison invented the light bulb. His success was not immediate. He had to find a filament that would last long enough to be marketable.

During his effort, having tried thousands of times, he was asked, "Mr. Edison, you have failed so many times. Are you discouraged?" Edison said, "No, I'm not discouraged, because I've not failed thousands of times. I've just found thousands of ways it doesn't work."

In January of 1991, having given a lecture in the Poconos, I was driving to the Newark airport, when I passed a sign for Thomas Edison's museum. I was early for my flight, a rare occurrence, and decided to visit this historic place. They told me that Edison failed 10,000 times before discovering a filament that would last long enough to be marketable. Rather than being discouraged, he always asked himself, "What did I do right so that the filament lasted as long as it did? Why did this filament last three minutes, and why did this one last nine minutes? Now, next time, how might I reach twelve?"

Today, because of Edison's attitude toward failure, we have the light bulb. We each need to recognize our attitude toward adversity. When the world is not all we hoped it would be, what do we think about? *Our thoughts determine our feelings*. If we think negatively when failing, we will too often feel depressed.

Feelings Determine Our Behavior

Often we are like children trying something new. If we fail and begin thinking of why we did badly, we might become like a critical parent to ourselves, compounding our feelings of inadequacy and reinforcing our doubts. Instead, if ever again we are disappointed by defeat, we want to be a positive parent to ourselves. We develop thoughts that guide our inner child through the difficult times.

When an experience is below our expectations, we often ask ourselves, "Why did I fail?" While this question might seem reasonable, our answers may only confirm our doubts. Thinking of why we did badly can cause us to forget our strengths, lose our enthusiasm and not want to try again. Dwelling on the reasons why we have performed below our expectations might also cause us to become depressed and defensive. If, when we fail, we congratulate ourselves for making the effort, rather than being disappointed, we will feel encouraged to try again.

As an example, a child returns from school with a bad report card. His mother, upset by his grades, tells him, "Take the card to your father." As he approaches his father, he wonders to himself, "Why have I done so badly? Possibly I have poor study habits, I don't really care about school, I am somewhat lazy and maybe I'm just not that smart." So he says, "Dad, here's my report card."

His father looks at his grades and says, "Obviously, son, you haven't been cheating."

The longer he evaluates the report card, the more upset he becomes. Finally he says, "You have terrible study habits, and you don't care about school."

The child no longer has any doubts in his mind. Now he is convinced that he lacks the ability and the intelligence. From then on, whenever he fails, he will probably say to himself, "I'm just lazy and stupid." If ever he were to succeed he might think, "How did that happen? I must have been lucky."

Mental Rehearsal

If we think back to our first job, we might remember how we felt as we traveled to the interview. We may have felt unprepared and insecure. Maybe, before we met our prospective employer, we found a quiet place for a few minutes of mental preparation. Using imagery, we visualized ourselves as the person we needed to be. Then we played the role, acting as though we were confident, and got the job.

Some of us might consider "role playing" to be inappropriate. We might feel that acting as though we are someone else is being superficial. If so, we should consider the value in playing a role until the characteristic becomes natural to us. We can all probably think back to when we were twelve years old and felt, in some way, inadequate. Possibly, we were inhibited in telling jokes or apprehensive when speaking in front of a group.

Then we remembered someone who had the quality we needed, such as a visiting relative or a teacher. Maybe we watched an actor or actress in a movie portraying the quality that we were lacking. We thought to ourselves, "If I were as uninhibited as this person, I might have more fun," or "If I were as confident, then I might gain more respect," so we began playing the role.

As we gained positive feedback, we thought to ourselves, "Maybe I have this quality." Then we integrated the quality into our self-image. The more attributes we incorporate into our personality, the more we have to draw from. Now, as the years pass, we may forget the origins of our qualities.

Whenever we feel disappointed by defeat, we first need to ask ourselves, "In what way have I succeeded?" Once I was helping my son with his multiplication table. He had never tried the entire table, so I tested him. He got thirty-seven wrong and twenty-nine right. He was feeling bad about his scores, so I explained to him, "You didn't get any wrong. You got twenty-nine right and discovered the thirty-seven that you have yet to learn. Think of how much time was required to learn the twenty-nine. With a little more effort you will learn all of of them. Be patient with yourself."

Just as we need to be a good parent to our children, so we need to be a good mother or father to our own inner child. We often have our feelings hurt by the negative feedback of others or by experiences that were less than what we expected. Remember Thomas Edison. *We guide ourselves through our frustrations* by first asking, "What did I do right?" Then we ask ourselves, "Next time how can I do even better?"

Responsibility and Maturity

As a young man, Joe Tracy went through a half dozen years of significant financial success in leasing. But, he relates how that changed:

> Suddenly, I was in a bad streak. One day I found myself on the verge of bankruptcy, divorced and alone. My only solution was a $35-per-month health club where I could shower and dress while living out of my car.

Self-destructive addictions were a factor in my downfall. In my worst moments I felt thoroughly depressed and would never have imagined myself being happy again. There were so many people that I could blame, but I decided to change my attitude and blame myself. It was time to take responsibility. Gradually, I began to recreate a positive momentum. I understand now that I would never have made the necessary changes if it wasn't for the bad times.

Often we are traveling at high speeds, the tension increasing throughout our day. Soon the intensity can become a serious problem. Changing our perception of what is causing the emotional pressure, such as finding the humor in the situation, can release all the anxiety.

> **Defeat, rather than disappointing us, stimulates our imagination.**

> **Thinking of new ways to succeed will increase our effort.**

> **Persevering will sharpen our skills.**

> **If we stay consistent, our results will usually be significant.**

> **Our thoughts determine our feelings.**

> **Experiencing the adventure creates real knowledge.**

> **Our feelings determine our behavior.**

7
Strengthen Self-Esteem

Accomplishing something of value enhances our self-esteem.

When our continent was first colonized by Europeans our society was agricultural. We were largely farmers and blacksmiths.

Then came the Industrial Revolution, which caused us to leave our farms and become factory workers. Today many of us, as factory and office workers, still work from nine until five in a confined and structured environment. We follow instructions and accept the authority of others.

For those who work in a factory, making a mistake can have very serious consequences. There is often no margin of error. If a worker does not follow instructions and do exactly what he or she is told to do, injury might be the result.

Becoming Entrepreneurial

Today a significant percentage of us do not work in factories. Rather than working on an assembly line, physically exerting ourselves, we are choosing to stretch ourselves mentally. We develop new applications for computers. We create complex products. We are entrepreneurs who are marketing unique services in a rapidly changing environment.

When we work in a factory, failure can mean losing an arm. When we become entrepreneurial, failure takes on an entirely new perspective. *Adversity becomes an arena for creativity.* Failure becomes a stimulant to innovate and go beyond old patterns.

Many of us have heard people say, "I have thirty years of experience." Too often they do not have thirty years of experience, but one day of experience and thirty years of repetition. When we work in a factory, we spend our first day learning how to operate a machine and the rest of our lives perfecting the process. When we take ownership of our own responsibilities, then we need to break out of old patterns. Our "factory mentality" needs to be replaced by a new thinking. Rather than following instructions, we need to *become self-disciplined* and *take the initiative in creating new strategies.*

The Realities of a New Environment

Phil Johnson, for many years, taught selling skills and coordinated training programs for Control Data Corporation, including the lectures I presented for his firm. CDC, well known as an innovative corporation, was willing to experiment and develop new products.

But, Control Data overlooked bottom-line profit and the changing dynamics in the market place. Soon CDC was losing its competitive position and in danger of bankruptcy. When a company is having difficulty making a profit, then one solution is to reduce costs. Downsizing, layoffs and austerity become the hard reality. Phil lost his job and, at that point, decided to become a consultant.

Initially, Phil developed a few clients and felt he was making progress. Yet the recession continued to affect his business. By the fall of 1991 Phil had lost his largest account. As the Minnesota weather turned to winter, Phil's economic circumstances also began to chill. His challenge was similar to that of literally a million other people. One of Phil's greatest strengths is his humility, which gives him the *courage to be honest.* He shared his thoughts on his predicament with me:

> Being a sales training consultant is a natural for me because of my years managing Control Data sales training. Yet, in reality, I dread making cold calls and would much rather be in the classroom instead of selling. The situation becomes even more difficult when my market is shrinking.
>
> There is also a tendency, when I am down, to turn my computer on and shut myself away. Working on my computer makes me feel productive even though I might be using it to avoid developing my

business. We all have to realize that the computer can save us or shelter us from our challenges. Sometimes you have another great idea to work on, but, at the end of the day, you haven't made a call or been productive.

When we are uncomfortable, we tend to focus on those activities that make us feel secure. While our strengths help us to succeed, they can also protect us from unfamiliar or threatening situations. When our ego is vulnerable, we may use our strengths as defense mechanisms. Successful people confront responsibilities that are uncomfortable as a way of developing new strengths and skills.

There is a basic thought process I revert to: that I am intelligent and need to keep thinking of ways through this maze. I have never lost my belief in myself. I am the same person I was when business was going well. I remind myself that if I continue to work hard, I will eventually succeed. Relearning can be monumental, but it also helps me to develop new opportunities.

Marketing today is like entering into an electronic jungle. Today's decision makers were born with television. They are conditioned to immediate stimulation, to getting their information from pictures and sound bites. Unfortunately, communicating and establishing rapport has often been reduced to impersonal fax machines and phone mail. Just getting through to talk to the right person can be overwhelming. Often the only answer is to break the objective into steps: leave a message, ask for an appointment, transfer to someone who can help, send information or ask the secretary for a time when the person might be available.

Phil reminds me of the constant challenge that we all confront when technological change is accelerating and we are in danger of becoming obsolete. We have the capacity to think, innovate and create new resources. We have to capitalize on what we develop or lose what we already have.

Achievement or Comfort

As I listened to Phil, I began to think of the conflicting needs within us. One need is to achieve something significant for our own self-respect. The other is to avoid failure so that we can stay comfortable. If we are committed to achievement, then we better be ready for possible failure. Otherwise we might be discouraged by defeat.

In reading Hamlet's classic speech, we are reminded of this inherent conflict and struggle:

> To be, or not to be, that is the question:
> Whether 'tis nobler in the mind to suffer
> The slings and arrows of outrageous fortune
> Or to take arms against a sea of troubles,
> And by opposing end them.

Many of us do not want "to suffer the slings and arrows of outrageous fortune." We just want to be comfortable.

The cartoon character Andy Capp sleeps on the couch during the day, while his wife Flo works. His evenings are devoted to drinking at the local pub and playing darts. In one particular cartoon he awakens on the couch for a moment and thinks to himself, "I'm bored. I'm flippin' bored. Of course Flo is never bored, but then Flo works. Maybe if I worked I wouldn't be bored either." He pauses, then realizes, "I guess I'll never find out."

When our primary desire is being comfortable, then we might be in danger of becoming bored and depressed. If we instead enjoy the challenge of achieving high expectations, we often may experience failure and become uncomfortable.

Fortunately, there is a way to succeed and still feel comfortable, no matter what happens. We merely need to stay *committed to our high expectations while learning how to deal with disappointment.* Even more important, if we thrive on failure, then any *adversity will actually accelerate our success.*

If we decide that being comfortable is most important, then we must make sure we never fail. Avoiding failure requires that we never try to succeed. Our lives will then become devoted to the monotony of doing tomorrow what we did yesterday. Never feeling the excitement of experiencing new adventures, we will soon become bored and depressed.

Failure Strengthens Our Ego

When we fail, we have a choice: We can allow the experience to cut at our ego and traumatize us, or create scar tissue that strengthens our ego so that we can more easily deal with disappointment.

I have always been inspired by the story of a nine-year-old boy, going to school on a bitter cold day in February of 1916. Glenn and his older brother, Floyd, arrived early at their one-room school house. When Floyd lit the wood in the stove, an explosion occurred, and both children were caught in flames. Though their bodies were badly burned, they were able to run back home. Their parents placed both in their own bed, and the doctor did the best he could.

Glenn watched as Floyd suffered for three months before he passed away. Six months later Glenn's body had healed well enough for him to be on crutches. The doctor explained that his leg muscles were so damaged that he would never walk on his own and that if he tried he would only experience horrible pain. On his first day on crutches, he decided to make the effort and collapsed in pain.

Yet, through his own determination and the encouragement of his family, Glenn continued to try. The effort was very difficult, but his muscles slowly strengthened, and the pain began to lessen. Gradually, Glenn walked again.

His next challenge was to be able to run. Each day he would go into the fields and, holding on to his horse's tail, be dragged along until he could run. Since he was unable to run as well as his friends, who called him "Scarlegs," each day he would run for miles. In his effort to recover from the fire, he became so resilient that, in 1934 in Princeton, New Jersey, Glenn Cunningham set the world's record for the mile.

Many of us have experienced tragedies such as the loss of a loved one. Tragedy in our personal life can change our perspective of business disappointments. Our failures diminish in magnitude and become manageable distractions. But, we can all develop a healthy perspective of reality without having to suffer through a personal loss.

Consider the heroic accomplishments of those who challenge themselves. The problem for too many of us is that we have yet to develop scar tissue on our ego. We lack the inner resiliency. Just as the heat of the furnace tempers steel, so the *intensities of life's experiences temper and strengthen our own ego.*

A grain of sand inside an oyster will cut the insides of the oyster, just as failure, rejection and anxiety can tear our insides. Of course, the oyster has the ability to convert the irritant into an object of beauty. Correspondingly, we can *convert our greatest frustrations into our greatest strengths.*

Weathering the Difficult Times

Marjie Hollinrake owns Zuma travel agency in Malibu. She told me her primary motivation in starting her own business was "being in control of my own destiny, making my own choices and decisions." Today the success that Marjie and her husband enjoy is the result of having weathered many difficult times. She recounted some of those:

> I was very close to my mother, and when she passed away, the wonderful memories became more important to me. When my son

reached thirty, a virus destroyed his insulin capacity. He developed diabetes and now requires two injections a day. While we were very upset, I kept reminding myself of the positive side, that there is at least a substance that keeps him alive. Not that long ago he wouldn't have survived. My husband also lost his job just as we had bought our new home. That was a real struggle, but we stayed optimistic, and the problem eventually passed by. Then we lost a significant sum of money because of an unscrupulous person. Someone stealing from you causes anger and hatred, but I continue to have faith in others. In spite of being shot down, *you have to keep moving into the future,* staying cautious of immobilization and *learning from your mistakes.*

Marjie and her husband, Jerry, know that when they are in the middle of a great disappointment, they will still have each other, their family and friends to help them through the bad times. Some of us develop our self-reliance, while some turn to others for help. Marjie allows the adversity to strengthen her self-sufficiency while still allowing strong relationships to be supportive. If we become purely self-reliant during the dark days, we are in danger of becoming an island unto ourselves. If we exclusively turn to people for help, we might become too dependent. Marjie commented on this:

> The balancing of both comes with maturity. I recognize that I am more a leader than a follower. As a leader you cannot live with negative feelings, particularly in business. When you are taking care of clients, your success is based on how responsive you are, on accepting and helping people. When a problem occurs, we have to stay patient and take their side.
>
> In 1991, I watched my business decline as people were staying home. During a recession you have to look forward. You put the bad times behind you. The only other choice is to feel miserable. You cannot let the past frustrations simmer within yourself. There is nothing to be gained by stewing in stress. Resolve the causes of your mistakes and move into the future. Otherwise, you become more nervous and never last.
>
> Recently, my resiliency was tested again when our house was destroyed by fire. I lost my art collection, crystal, photographs and family antiques that were part of my life. It was very hard at first, being devastated and knowing how much my husband and children were also hurt by all we lost. But neighbors insisted we stay with them, and friends had a "fire party" and we received 200 gifts to replace the necessities. Then we began making plans for our new home, and the challenge became fun and exciting. We have an opportunity to create a new design on the old foundation and make it better than it was.

Somehow the loss of a home, which for most of us would be more disturbing than the loss of a job, becomes symbolic. When we experience a loss, we need to look forward to rebuilding. Though we might, at first, be devastated, we convert our unhappiness into an adventure. We think of how to improve on what we had. We allow the stress of the situation to help us become more self-reliant while still turning to others for help as a way of recovering more quickly. Every loss leaves us with an empty place to be filled by our imagination. We need the courage to create something of greater value.

Fire and Fear

Probably the first invention, even before the wheel, was fire. It ignited wood into flames, which took away the darkness, created warmth on a cold night and protected us from predators.

Fear was, perhaps, our first emotion. We were frightened by predators or the thought of freezing to death in a winter storm. Even darkness frightened us.

Just as fire transforms the energy of a dead tree into warmth, light and protection, so *our fears ignite us.* They create energy that can prepare us for danger before it arrives, stimulate us to take action, and keep us moving when we are exhausted.

Fire and fear can save us. They can also consume and destroy us. We need to harness the energy and channel it into a creative force for achievement.

Adversity is an arena for creativity.

Take the initiative in developing new strategies.

Diminish our failures by breaking them into manageable parts.

Difficult times strengthen our self-sufficiency.

Our fears can ignite our creative energy.

8
Become More Resilient

Imagine all the possibilities in our lives.

Taking Chances

Fifteen years ago Mark McKinney became impaired by arthritis of his spine, though he does not consider himself handicapped. As he explained, "Some people have brown eyes, and some blue. I have something that most people do not have." Mark does admit that his disability affected him, first physically, then psychologically:

> I no longer could physically do what I had enjoyed when I was younger. This frustration began to affect my image of myself in other areas of my life. I felt I had aged, and I began to baby myself. I became more protective and developed this desire to be easier on myself. I stopped challenging myself as a way of avoiding stress.

Mark is a stockbroker with Dean Witter Reynolds, Inc., and by late 1990, his income had dropped below the company's minimum standard. He was notified, in early 1991, that if he did not multiply his revenue, then, reluctantly, management would have no choice but to terminate him at the end of the year. As the months passed Mark continued in the same pattern. Nothing was changing, and Mark was further behind his required objective. In June he and I had a four-hour meeting. Later he remembered it this way:

> As I drove to our meeting, I was convinced that there was no solution. I did not want to admit that I was a loser, but I believed that my situation was impossible. Yet if my vice-president asked me to block out a few hours [to go to the meeting], I would at least listen, even though I could never expect to make such a huge increase in my income.

Six months later, during the Christmas holidays, Mark called to tell me, "I've tripled my income, received an $8500 bonus and saved my job. It's miraculous." Mark then discussed what he had done to assure his success:

> The change began with one idea—that I needed to open my mind to all the possibilities. As long as we do not believe we have a chance, we will be mentally blind to all the ways we can succeed. Since I was going to lose my job, there could be no additional harm in playing a mental game of believing that I could succeed and seeing if any solutions would come to me.

If we decide that there is no hope, then we will usually miss the opportunities available to us. If we are convinced that we can succeed, we might be surprised to find our subconscious creativity providing us with innovative solutions.

All of us have had the experience of forgetting something, such as someone's name. As long as we keep trying, we become more frustrated, which only blocks our mind from accessing the information. We succeed when we stop trying and turn the problem over to our subconscious mind. Suddenly, the answer comes to us. Mark experienced this:

> The first solution that came to me was that I needed to be a child again, taking chances. Rather than working more hours, I needed to demand more of myself. I made a decision to compete with myself. I would make the extra prospecting call today instead of tomorrow, as well as trying for one more appointment.

Competing with Ourselves

Self-competition can shield us from failure and frustration. As Mark began to compete with himself, he developed an immunity to rejection. The game was to improve his previous day's efforts. If he could score one more call or one more appointment, he was assuring the positive momentum that would drive him toward his target. He relayed how he did this:

> I set a minimum goal for myself each day of how much I would earn. Then I would try to surpass that level. Competing with myself converted my challenge into a game, and any anger I confronted just seemed to pass me by.

Mark's success reminded me that I have always responded well to self-competition. Whether in improving my performance in the Boston Marathon, making quota at IBM or developing my lecture business, I have discovered that competing with myself creates a number of benefits.

We know that our activities create our results. Therefore, we *place value on the activities that can assure our results. We focus our mind on performing beyond our previous effort* and disregard any peripheral distractions that might otherwise frustrate us.

Too often we become discouraged by people who are doing better than we are. We also can lose motivation by observing those who are not doing as well as we are, as though they are bringing us down. Instead, we should become intrigued with surpassing yesterday's performance.

First, we decide what we wish to accomplish. Then, we need to determine the activities that will create our desired results. If we keep score of our activity and try to exceed yesterday's points, we can create a momentum that can assure our success.

Beginning Again

There was one last idea that Mark shared with me. In addition to the specific technique of self-competition, he spoke of no longer being passive:

> I realized that I was okay just the way I was. I just needed to be more of myself. I have always been considerate of people, but inhibited by a fear of rejection. I was often reluctant to extend myself, for fear that people would not reciprocate. Gradually I came to understand that I could be aggressive without being abrasive. All I needed to do was focus my efforts on helping people. Actively helping people is productive. My self-image is no longer of a person so sensitive as to be cautious and protective. More importantly I understand why I have tripled my income and this awareness is keeping me consistent.

Last week I received a note from Mark:

> Currently, I continue to experience success, and my business is run-

ning 15 percent ahead of my goal for the period. As a result, I feel a rebirth of the competitive spirit from my youth.

Mark is no longer a young man, but he is growing again. He reminds us that change can be as simple as making a decision that, regardless of how hopeless our situation might seem, *we can capitalize on our strengths and begin again.*

> **Successful people have a different perception of reality.**

When Mark changed his image of himself, of who he was and what he could accomplish, his results changed. We all need to understand the relationship between the expectations we have of ourselves and our perceptions of reality.

High expectations motivate us to succeed. We may become discouraged by the first defeat if we interpret our failure as a negative experience and a reason to quit. Rather than lower our expectations we need to change our perceptions of reality.

> **Failure is only an experience that was less than we expected.**

What if we changed our attitude toward failure and decided that failure did not exist? What if we perceived failure, not as failure, but only as an experience that was less than we expected? What if we imagine that there was a benefit to every experience that was less than we expected? Then failure would become like a trampoline. We would automatically bounce back from every fall.

Rather than be disappointed, failure can actually accelerate our success. Whenever we think we have failed, we merely change our view of what happened. For example, we can decide that *failure makes us more resilient.*

Failure can make us weaker or stronger. The choice is ours. Too often we unconsciously select the negative alternative. We allow the disappointment to "tear us down." Instead we want the "bad times" to strengthen our ego.

Making Decisions

Mike Lombardo is ranked in the top 5 percent in production among 200 Graebel Van Line salespeople. Mike has just been promoted to vice-president of the East Coast region. Recently, on a warm, sunny day in February, I was sitting poolside, speaking with Mike in his home in Florida. I asked him if he ever had a bad day in his life. His story began in 1982:

> I was living in New Jersey, and I had just lost my father. Immediately after his death my business wiped out. Everything was crashing in on me. I had no money, and my wife and I were wondering how we would feed the children. My emotions were working against me, and psychologically I was at an all-time low. I felt caught in the confusion of life as though I was looking in a mirror that had become clouded and I couldn't find myself.
>
> My turning point began with a decision. I had to start thinking, not of what I was doing wrong, but of what I do best. I put the negatives out of my mind and went into the transportation business. I had no experience but I recognized the opportunity. Some people thought I was crazy because I knew nothing about the business, but I knew I had the ability to sell and that was all that was important.
>
> My success was not automatic. For the first six months I made very little, and my wife and I had a difficult time financially at Christmas. She was worried, but I told her, "Carolyn, I've had a good learning year. Next year I'll have a good money year," and I did.
>
> Every day you win and lose, so you allow the negatives to make you sharper and wiser. If I lose a big order, then I stop, do some soul searching and then return with a vengeance. Losing is like pouring gas on a fire. Losing makes me better. I doubt I would be as good if I always won. I almost welcome the negative on occasion because it helps me. Losing, from time to time, makes me hungry. If your business always goes your way, you become complacent.
>
> I never forget the bad times, for they renew my determination to stay motivated and in control. If I want something badly enough, whether I am an auto mechanic or selling pencils, the more I put into it, the more I will get out of it. Even now I keep myself on the edge by reminding myself, "I am only as good as my last sale."
>
> Every morning I look in the mirror and remind myself, "I am the best." My attitude is very simple: I will sell the account, and if I don't, I will still make a friend, build a relationship and eventually get the contract. Success is based on a mind set—"I know I can do it!"

Mike illustrates the power of positive affirmation. Our thoughts determine our feelings. *As we think, so shall we feel.* Our thoughts must be in tune with reality. We turn the dial on the radio until we are in tune with the station. In the same way we tune our thoughts in our head until we create the desired energy.

But, if our thoughts are going to produce the desired emotions, they must be definite and strong. When our thoughts are vague, our emotions will be vague. The more confident our thoughts, the more sure we will feel in taking control of the challenges we confront.

Creative Visualization

Our success begins with *a decision, of where we want to be* in the future. Then we phrase our thoughts in the present tense. Rather than saying to ourselves, "I hope that, if I try, I will succeed," we sell ourselves on the idea that "I am doing it now because I deserve the success." Even a negatively phrased thought such as "I never procrastinate because I hate to waste time" is positive. Mike commented on visualizing success:

> I believe in creative visualization. Whenever I have a problem I know where I'll find the solution. *The answer is always in the mirror.* When I see myself as the person I need to be, then people will see me the same way. We need to become a magnet that attracts positive energy.

This is a key factor in our success. Mike does not say to himself, "I'd like to be the best," or "I am trying to be the best." Rather, he says to himself, "I am the best." Though Mike is totally focused before his presentation and tells himself, "There is no way that I'm not going to succeed," he also thinks of reality—"that I may not succeed." He balances his confidence with the realization that "I may not have all the answers, but I will be one step toward getting the account."

> Disengage from thinking in absolutes, of failure or success, as though our world was either black or white.

We rarely fail totally or succeed completely. Rather *our failures are filled with success,* and our successes are usually touched by some degree of failure. Rather than believing that we are either winning or losing as though there is no in between, we need to see the experience for what it really is. We need to *find success within our failures.*

Greg Wood is a manager for a major stockbrokerage firm. Today he is happy and successful, but he has not always had positive momentum, nor has his success happened spontaneously. He told his story to me:

> Neither my decline nor my return was entirely by design. Most of what I am accomplishing is because of what I have already suffered through in the past. I'll never forget my ex-wife driving off with our children and her boyfriend in my new Mercedes. I am a very visual person, and I can still see the dirt blowing in my face as she drove away. In that moment I made a decision between pitying myself or getting on with my life. My decision created a design that automatically helps me today.

Ever since, whenever I feel I have fallen into one of the potholes of life, I remember that the solution can be very simple: just concentrate on what I need to do. Focus and do it. Through the ups and downs I remember that I am the only one who can help myself.

I have developed this fatalistically positive philosophy that every bad experience is only positioning me for a better situation. When someone kicks me in the stomach and I double over, I usually discover there was a bullet aimed at my head, which just missed me.

Greg reminds us that what motivates one person toward success can distract someone else. Some of us do better by depending on people, such as support groups, while others of us are more effective by becoming self-reliant. I relate to Greg. I enjoy snowshoeing alone in the High Sierras, speaking to a different audience each day and finding a moment of solitude at sunset. Other people need people to stay on target. Greg continued his thoughts:

Being a visual person causes me to feel as though I can create an out-of-body experience, as though I am looking at myself. Then I can see myself objectively and more easily make intelligent decisions.

During my last down cycle, when my income dropped with the stock market and my weight jumped fifteen pounds, I had to play the mental game again. Creating a design for success begins with the decision that I will no longer participate in the negative nonsense. I begin with an exercise program and lose the weight. From then on the process is instinctive.

Greg knows that success or failure in one part of life can affect any other part. When we are not exercising, we might gain weight, which may slow us down in the job, which would cause us frustration that can negatively affect love relationships, which can be damaging to our self-image, causing a loss of self-esteem, resulting in depression or anger. Self-discipline can reverse the cycle. We never allow failure to negatively affect our momentum. Instead we create positive experiences and regain control of our lives.

Rewarding Ourselves

Greg talked about rewarding himself:

All my successes begin with a decision that I don't want bad things happening to me. Ninety percent of the game is mental, beginning with the way I change my perceptions. Then there are times when success occurs only from hard work.

I recently bought a new car as a reward for what I had accomplished. I also call people I know who have just experienced some significant success and congratulate them. There is no time for psychological self-mutilation. I create personal rewards along the way, for being on schedule. I give myself a gift. Too many people play a pity game. By rewarding ourselves we strengthen our self-image. We remind ourselves that we deserve to succeed.

Believing we have a chance to succeed sharpens our mental vision.

Our subconscious mind can provide us with innovative solutions.

Surpassing yesterday's success can create a positive momentum.

Knowing why we are successful can assure our consistency.

There is a direct relationship between our perceptions of what we think we can accomplish and our eventual results.

Failure makes us more resilient.

Rewarding ourselves with gifts creates the desired incentives.

Find the success within the failures.

9
Establish Successful Patterns

We use the energy of our fears to propel us into the creative process.

Fear and Creativity

One day, in the summer of 1984, Jack Matson, a professor of engineering at the University of Houston, was playing tennis. Storm clouds appeared, but Jack continued playing. Suddenly, he was hit by lightning.

> I was not damaged physically, but I felt I had nearly died. I was so damaged psychologically that I needed therapy. As part of the counseling, I found that my creativity was blocked.
>
> Thirteen months after my traumatic experience, the university asked me to develop and teach a course in creativity. There had been a lack of originality among our students. We agreed that the process the students were going through needed to evolve beyond learning into creating new technology, so that they could experience product development.
>
> Although the initial semester was a disaster, I persisted. The first success began with popsicle sticks. The objective was to build the tallest structure. Those students who allowed themselves the most mistakes usually succeeded. Those students who rigidly followed their first idea most frequently were the losers. Failure is an essential part of the learning experience. *Only through trial and error can we map the unknown.*

Success as a Two-Step Process

The first step to success is to know every path available to reach our destination. We allow ourselves to be a searchlight by moving in all imaginable directions. The second step is *being single-minded.* We focus all of our energy into a single obsession. Yet the only way to discover which target to focus on begins with flexibility. Only then can we decide *which path offers the greatest opportunity with the least risk.* The strategy is to *get through the failure as quickly as possible.*

One step in this process requires *an exploration of our inner selves. We use the energy of our fears to propel us into the creative process.* Unfortunately, too many people allow the negative energy of their fears to inhibit their creativity. The number of failures we have then determines how successful we are going to be. Success requires becoming a daily risk taker. Too often we ask ourselves, "Who needs this?"

> **The faster we innovate the more competitive we become.**

We need to shorten the development cycle if we are to quicken the delivery schedule. Those companies that accelerate the process gain a competitive advantage. Being on the leading edge, as opposed to dragging along in the rear, depends on our flexibility rather than our rigidness. This is based on whether or not we accept risk. Our ability to change begins with *our appreciation of failure as part of the developmental cycle* of engineering new technology.

We need to develop new strategies and strengths. This requires experimenting and trying new techniques. The results can often be disappointing, but we never truly fail. We might be disappointed by defeat, but we understand how adversity improves our chance of succeeding.

Patterns for Success

We feel secure with our habits and skills. Whether we are a bank manager, tax accountant or computer programmer, we often feel insecure when making a presentation or asking a prospective client for a decision. Taking on greater responsibility can be difficult. The unfamiliar can be frightening. We might stumble, make mistakes or feel embarrassed.

We tie our shoes and drive a car without thinking. We leave home in the morning without apprehension. Yet each of us can think back to a time in which we felt frustrated learning how to tie our shoes or nervous during our first driving lessons. We might also remember feeling a sense of panic when leaving home for our first day of school.

We often feel like children when we are facing our fears, whether in dealing with aggressive people, attempting downhill skiing for the first time or giving a speech. We need to attack our fears and establish success patterns. This requires a five-step process:

1. First, determine or acknowledge the fear that is immobilizing us.
2. Second, tell people what is upsetting us, which helps to release the fear.
3. Third, decide how we can quit if the effort becomes too frustrating so we know we have control of the situation.
4. Fourth, begin slowly so we can feel our way into the challenge and reduce the danger of panic.
5. Fifth, imagine ourselves in a happy place so the fear is superseded by positive emotions.

Soon making a presentation will be as easy as driving a car, confronting negative people as automatic as tying our shoes and taking on a new physical activity as effortless as leaving home in the morning.

Creating a Stronger Self-Image

Over the years my children have traveled with me on my lecture tours, often one at a time, to have my sole attention. On one trip my daughter, Renee, sat in the back of the room and heard me speak for the first time. Afterwards she said to me, "Dad, I know who you are, and that was not you speaking up there; but that person was sincere, so if that person is real, but not you, then who are you?"

Her confusion reminded me of how I have developed my personality. Usually, when I have tried to reach a new level of success, I have discovered that I lacked an important quality. The determination to achieve my objective forced me to persevere until I finally developed the necessary strengths. In actuality I am creating another dimension within my personality. Each development increases my ability to succeed in another area of business.

If we confront our fears, we can create a stronger self-image. Our new sense of identity then becomes like a building block, adding to who we are and what we are capable of achieving.

On the other hand, if we do not resolve our apprehensions, we may never grow beyond our present position. Our challenge is to confront our vulnerabilities and establish a new sense of confidence. What we achieve causes us to become more than we have ever been before.

We can then feel confident taking on leadership responsibilities. People will feel comfortable depending on us for advice and following our recommendations. We can be a friend with our children or give a dynamic speech. We can be anyone we want to be because we have developed these separate identities. As we create these strengths, our fears dissipate, people respect us and we gain self-esteem.

In 1978 I took my nephew with me to Maui for a lecture I was giving for a stockbrokerage firm's convention. Jay sat in the back of the room, and the session went very well. Afterwards, as we were leaving, Jay asked, "Uncle Art, are you always this good?"

I said, "Yes, Jay, except when I give a banquet speech. Often the group, after a long day of meetings and a cocktail party, have had too much to drink and are tired. Then there is the announcement that there is a motivational speaker. Some sessions have been so difficult that I can't guarantee my usual super performance."

I realized as I was talking to Jay that, if I felt this way, I should not do this type of speech. At that moment I decided I would never again be a banquet speaker. He then asked, "How much do you get paid for a dinner speech?" When I told him, his immediate reaction was, "Uncle Art, I'd be glad to make a fool of myself for that much money."

I thought to myself, "He's right. I'm taking myself too seriously. This is just one more opportunity to sharpen my skills and become more effective."

Many years have passed since Jay's comment, and today I frequently give banquet speeches, and no matter how difficult the situation, I always do well. The times in which I have failed and felt embarrassed have motivated me to develop a repertoire of approaches to deal with even the most challenging audiences.

Before I give a lecture I assume that I will give a great presentation, but I take nothing for granted. We each need to find the balance between believing we will succeed and acknowledging that we might fail. In this way we prepare ourselves for any possible difficulties while still feeling confident.

Assume that we will do well, but take nothing for granted.

Being on the Edge

There are many similarities between taking on new challenges in business and our first downhill skiing trip:

1. It is a cold world out there.
2. We can fail in spectacular ways.
3. We can experience humiliation.

First we are taught to snowplow, in which we move into a contorted position, our knees and feet turned inward. This technique helps us stay in control, so we ski slowly and feel secure. Next, we learn to move sideways up a slope, and then snowplow back down.

Once we have mastered this lesson, we are ready for our first lift ride. Our instructor shows us the correct way to sit and hold on to our poles. As the lift carries us upward, we are exhilarated by views of snow-covered pine trees and granite walls. Then comes the moment to get off the chair. We ask the person alongside us, "When do they stop this thing?" We feel a sense of panic when we are told it's not going to stop, thinking to ourselves, "How will I get off this continuously moving object?"

Afterwards, they stop the lift so people can drag us out of the way. These people then find our gloves, poles and hat, and help us put on our skis, while Japanese skiers take pictures of us. We now shuffle over to the beginning of the "bunny slope." A few minutes earlier, when at the bottom of the hill, we looked upward and exclaimed, "What's the big deal? This is almost flat." Now, standing at the top, we feel as though we are at the edge of a cliff.

We position ourselves into the snowplow and carefully begin skiing downhill, until we take our first fall. As we lie in the cold, wet snow, watching one of our skis sliding into the wilderness while six-year-old children without poles whiz past us, we may develop a great desire to be back in the warm lodge.

If we think of why we are doing badly, we may only convince ourselves to spend the remainder of our ski trip in the Jacuzzi. Instead, like Thomas Edison, we think about what we are doing right. We appreciate how much we have learned in just three hours. We also congratulate ourselves on having the courage to confront our fears. Once we realize why we are doing so well, we can then ask ourselves, "What will I ask my instructor, on the bottom of this hill, that will reduce my falls from twelve this time to only seven next time?"

> **We cannot fail.**

Maybe the experience was not all that we had hoped it would be, but we first ask ourselves, "What did I do right so that I got as far as I did?" Once we have answered that question, we then can ask ourselves, "Next time what will I do in order to last even longer?"

Whether making a presentation, contacting prospective clients or skiing downhill for the first time, we want to remember that *failing frequently* teaches us how to maneuver. Taking small steps by starting on the beginners' ski slope minimizes the danger of falling. If we imagine ourselves succeeding before we try, we may also replace some of our apprehension with new confidence.

We envision our future, anticipate the crisis and create new stratas of confidence.

Only through trial and error can we map the unknown.

We create power and precision by focusing all of our energy into a single obsession.

We appreciate failure as part of the process of developing our potential.

We break procrastination by attacking our fears.

10
Play
the
Percentages

> We are remembered in life, not for how few times we fail,
> but for how often we succeed.

Babe Ruth swung in a way that has not been duplicated for decades, with the possible exception of Reggie Jackson. The Babe swung so hard that, when he missed, he would often fall down. Using our imagination, we can see him, having just fallen down, struck out, covered with dirt and walking back to the dugout, being booed by thousands. At that moment he would tip his cap to the fans, and when he hit a home run, he would also tip his cap to the fans.

What does a man think of, when being booed by thousands, that he can still tip his cap to the fans? He has come to understand, "I must fail a great deal in order to succeed." How often must any one of us fail in order to achieve our objectives? How many times must we strike out in order to hit a home run?

Babe Ruth was famous for having hit a total of 714 home runs. Few of us know that he also had 1,330 strikeouts. Why is it true that we remember his 714 home runs, but so few of us remember the number of strikeouts? The secret of success is understanding that *we are remembered in life, not for how few times we fail, but for how often we succeed.* Each of us know of people who work very hard to make sure they don't fail. Of course, they hardly ever do, but then they rarely succeed.

We all need to develop and crystallize our philosophy of success into a single thought that keeps us on track. If we keep our mind focused on our target, we will not be distracted by peripheral irritations.

Constantly Experiment

Success positions us for even greater challenges in which we increase the danger of misfortune. Our success might create so much confidence as to blind us to possible disaster. We want our fears to prepare us for the unpredictable. Then we can persevere through the storm. In this way we will continue to mature. As an illustration, Bruce Mulhearn, a California realtor for thirty years with twenty-five offices, relayed the following to me:

> February 8, 1981, will be known to me forever as "Black Sunday." I was returning from Lake Tahoe where I had just finished building condominiums. Interest rates had just reached 18 percent, and most of my buyers were canceling. It was the tip of the iceberg since all my developments were in trouble. We were building expensive homes in San Clemente, condominiums in Lakewood, housing in Phoenix, and ski units in Nevada. The world was falling in around my ears. My real estate company had over twenty branches.
>
> Helplessly, I watched as most of my 500 sales people ran out of money and had to seek employment elsewhere. I was closing offices as quickly as possible, while the losses were draining my remaining resources. We publicized that we were consolidating our offices for efficiency, which seemed an appropriate euphemism for survival. Every day I had painful interviews with loyal senior associates and managers who were leaving.
>
> I was in the middle of losing $3 million. It didn't take a mental genius to realize that I couldn't last much longer. One friend asked me about my physical and mental health. These were times of torment. I am not one for medication, but I could have done a sincere commercial for Alka Seltzer. It was devastating to see a twenty-year business going up in smoke.

> **Our sense of purpose can help us to continue striving through the bleakest of times.**

My physical exercise program of daily running and swimming helped me keep my sanity. I truly believe without the consistency of vigorous heart stimulation, my health would have been affected. I had the additional pressure of counseling longtime fellow realtors who had lost everything. My wife and family really cared for me and were at their best when things were at their worst. Trying to motivate those around me took its toll. There was nothing but stress and strain at the office. The one real pleasure I had was looking forward to evenings at home. Survival is the first requirement of a company. No matter how bleak the outlook, you always need to strive for some kind of goal.

> **There is a way of thinking that can resolve anxiety attacks.**

My longtime legal friend suggested the option of throwing in the towel. Cash in what chips remained and fly off to England. The very idea of giving in was totally foreign to all that had previously motivated me and a contradiction of all the principles I had stood for. Being positive had always been my long suit. I admit that I fantasized the concept of starting fresh and leaving my responsibilities and burdens behind. It would have been very easy to do. Anxiety attacks plagued my outlook. I knew that negative thoughts would mean my downfall. All they foster are more of the same until it becomes a whirlpool, pulling one to the bottom.

> **We create the magic that reverses the downfall.**

In the past, I humorously maintained that I was the worst person in the world to talk about the realism of our economy. Regardless of what stared me in the face, if I was asked about business, I would always respond with how great it was. I would then proceed with a detailed explanation of why I felt that way.

I admit that I'm more cautious now when asked the same question, but I still emphasize that business success will always be up to the individual. In the worst of times, the professional can make ideas work. You can pull rabbits out of the hat if you're totally committed.

There I was, mired in a myriad of problems—I quit calling them challenges early in 1981. What did I do besides wring my hands? I made some tough decisions, not all of them correct. Liquidity was my main concern. Without it, I wouldn't be able to survive. Sell at all costs was my motto. I sold, traded and bartered away properties that had severe negative cash flows. There was a great deal of time devoted to negotiating with bankers and loan representatives. In some cases, total equities were lost. The psychological burden was tremendous. These same ventures had looked outstanding in the late seventies. No one ever suspected the market would take such a long and deep downturn. Even the top economists predicted it would last no more than one year. Subsequently, we were all sadly shocked.

Constant experimentation can help us survive the worst of times.

In reflection, I can't believe the miracles that occurred. The many years of management experience, training and creativity were given their severest test. Never have the hours been longer, the concentration more intense, the commitment more complete. We pulled through the worst of it. We continuously experimented.

Anything is possible if you devote all your being and all your attention to it.

In 1983, we were helped a great deal by falling interest rates. How gratifying to be able to have the staying power until that occurred. Although we appear to be out of the woods today, the experience will never be forgotten. I learned many lessons. Perhaps the most important is the reinforcement of my previous belief that the need not to fail is a powerful stimulant. I could not visualize walking away with my tail between my legs. No matter how tempting it was, quitting was never in the cards.

Our ability to rebound from defeat during periods of adversity usually originates from our childhood.

After the Second World War, my father manufactured and bottled a liquid bleach in Newcastle, England. At the tender age of 8, I was selling it door to door. Saturdays were our busiest days. Saturday was also the day for Little League Soccer. I loved to play that game. The soccer matches were scheduled in the afternoon. In canvassing, I was not a volunteer—dad needed the help. How could I participate in the game when he required my assistance?

My father built a four-wheel cart, equipped with a container to hold twelve bottles of bleach. He dropped me off in a residential neighborhood over a mile from home. If I sold the bleach, I had the right to play soccer. I never missed a game.

I learned to focus on the positive. My objective was the game. The adversity of turndowns was tough, but I learned to separate myself from the selling of bleach. I told myself I wasn't being rejected—my product was. Besides, not everyone said "no." The reward of playing was a much finer reward than any punishment I felt from turndowns. It only required *discipline to concentrate on the goal.*

> Losing is part of the game of winning.

Be Willing to Fail

As I listened to Bruce I was reminded of all the great people who, only by failing frequently, were able to set records. I thought of Ty Cobb, a great baseball player. One of his many abilities was base stealing. In his single best year, he stole ninety-six bases in one hundred thirty-four tries. Correspondingly, few of us remember Max Carey of the Pittsburgh Pirates who, in 1922, stole fifty-one bases in fifty-three tries. Why is it true that we are familiar with Ty Cobb, but so few of us know Max Carey? Again, we are remembered, not for how few times we fail, but how often we succeed.

Many years ago in New York, I met Lou Brock who, at the time, held the record for stolen bases. He had set the record at about thirty-five. I asked him, "Young players are fast with quick reflexes. How do you explain setting such a record past your prime?"

He said, "Art, when you start out in baseball, you're young and you have the speed and reflexes. However, when you try to steal second base and you get thrown out, it's a long walk back to the dugout, with 40,000 fans watching you. When you reach my age, you come to understand that records are not set by being the quickest, but by the willingness to look bad in the eyes of others."

> We resolve our fears by taking risks.

> By confronting our fears, we create a stronger self-image.

11
React Like a Winner

> **We can establish new skills that replace old feelings of inadequacy.**

When striving for success, we will find ourselves in one of three patterns:

- We might take failure and rejection too much to heart and, under considerable stress, stop trying. We may even seek comfortable situations and compromise our expectations.

- Our high expectations may motivate us to persevere until we eventually succeed. Unfortunately, even though we are achieving our objectives, we may also take failure and rejection too personally, causing anxiety. The result is, though we have become prosperous, we are emotionally dissatisfied.

- Ideally, we have high expectations that motivate us to persevere until we succeed. More importantly, we develop unique reactions to failure, rejection and anxiety, in the absence of which we become bored and restless. We each need to decide what those reactions might be so we are inspired to take the necessary action.

Inspiration and Action

Joe Nuckols is the owner and founder of the first twenty-four-hour-a-day motivational radio station. I asked Joe if he ever had a bad day in his life:

Never. Events happen, but you don't write off the day. If something bad happens you learn from it and move on.

When I was nine years old, I wanted to be in radio. I would pretend to be a disk jockey on the hi-fi, which would drive my family crazy. I began working in radio at fourteen, but in the spring of 1975 I was out of work. It was a recessionary period. Not wanting to switch careers, I became absorbed in reading motivational books and doing mental exercises that required writing a success thought each day. My most significant motto was simply "Do it Now!" Regardless of how you feel, you must never procrastinate. If you are constantly moving toward your objective you maximize your chances of succeeding.

> **We must explore the possibilities of our intuition.**

I decided to listen to my intuition. I felt some instinctive need to break out and do it. My inner voice said, "Put all your possessions in storage and start driving." It was June 2, and I started driving south, driven by some need to be on the move. I would listen to radio stations, believing someone out there needed me. I came across one station that had an off-the-wall format and no consistency. I believed I could help them, and I made the call.

> **Finding people who need us can often assure our success.**

It was like a miraculous coincidence. The general manager was new in his job and needed a program manager. It was perfect. If I had been traveling two weeks later, I would have lost the opportunity. When you are hit with an inspiration, never procrastinate. Do it now!

> **Failure sharpens our senses.**

I worked for six years in that job, moving from program manager to sales manager to general manager. That experience made it possible for me to purchase my own station. I believe every adversity gives us an energy charge and helps us recognize what we otherwise would have never seen. Failure stops you in your tracks and makes you pay attention. I believe that if one door closes another one opens.

> **We find value in adversity.**

Too many times we are taught that, if we make a mistake, we should just move on, declare bankruptcy or get divorced, but I believe we never should give up on our beliefs. Our beliefs are a powerful force that help us make sense of all of our adversities. As Thomas Edison said, "Many of life's failures are those who gave up too soon."

Reactions

Whether we win or lose, are loved or rejected, or experience elation or depression is not based on luck or astrology. Rather, these results are a by-product of *our reactions,* which are dictated by our *perceptions* of reality, originating from our *expectations.*

There is a strong relationship between our *expectations* and our *ego resiliency.* If we have high expectations, we will persevere in order to fulfill our aspirations. If our egos are resilient, we will do better under pressure and capitalize on any difficulty.

Let's consider some less desirable circumstances. What will happen if our ego is resilient, but we do not expect much of ourselves? While we may have the resiliency to deal with difficult times, we may not feel a need to try. We might also be easily satisfied with minimum success and have little desire to develop our potential. We may even become complacent and disregard existing opportunities.

Then there are those of us who have high expectations, but lack ego resiliency. We are oversensitive. If our expectations are the more dominant influence in our lives, we will persevere, but suffer greatly when experiencing defeat or the unkindness of others. If our oversensitivity is a greater influence, then we might decide that the effort is too painful and sacrifice our expectations. Such a reaction might reduce stress, but in compromising our expectations, we often experience a loss of self-esteem, causing deeper frustration.

Staying committed to our high expectations will help us capitalize on existing opportunities, develop our talents and feel the excitement of taking on new challenges. Developing ego resiliency helps us persevere when we fail, we are rejected. It helps us use anxiety productively. Then we increase the chances of our negative experiences assuring our success. In this way we achieve our expectations while further strengthening our egos.

Feelings

Our reactions determine our *feelings*. Happiness or frustration do not occur as spontaneously as some of us might believe. Feelings do not originate from what happens to us, but from our reactions.

> If we change our reactions, we can change the way we feel.

One Saturday afternoon in October of 1962, the Grove City College football team was playing a game at home against their archrivals, Westminster. Grove City was ranked as one of the best defensive teams in the nation. The fans were thoroughly enjoying their anticipated victory. With less than two minutes to go, Grove City was leading seven to six.

Art Mitchell was playing for Grove City. When he snapped the ball it sailed well above the kicker's outstretched arms, rolling into the end zone for a two-point safety. The game ended in an 8-7 defeat, and Art was devastated. As one of the key players, he knew his team depended on him. The headline in the newspaper the next morning read, "Mitchell: The Goat of Westminster." In spite of his terrible error, he returned the following year and was selected team co-captain. He commented on his thoughts about the incident:

> Regardless of having failed, I still believed I was a winner. Having failed did not mean I was a failure. As much as I was emotionally devastated by the experience, I refused to allow it to affect my self-image. It is one thing to be devastated, but something else to be destroyed. Failure does not have to psychologically kill you. Though devastated and experiencing emotional pain, we can still believe we can succeed and therefore persevere. When we are destroyed there is nothing left of our ego and we seek only the comfortable path of security.

Art reminds us that we need to separate a humbling experience from our own sense of value. We cannot assume that just because we did badly we are no longer worthwhile. If we are human, then failure will upset us, but if we are objective, the experience will not take away our self-respect. Art continued:

> After college I joined IBM. I had learned that at any point in time you can fail. Whether on the athletic field or the business field, you have the opportunity to win or lose. The contest is only a game. Your attitude determines how you play, whether you take the game so seriously that you can't deal with defeat or stay at a peak effort, regardless of what happens.

> Recovering quickly from failure prepares us for our next contest.

In professional football, eight teams compete in the playoffs. Only two make the Super Bowl. If you lose, you have to wait until next year, and the defeat can cause a long winter of despair. In marketing you only have to wait until the next appointment to compete again. You could be notified at ten o'clock that you just lost a client, but, with an appointment in an hour, you have to recover. You have to be prepared and confident to take the necessary steps. One thought keeps you going—that losing does not make you a loser. You may have lost, but you can still be a winner.

After twenty years of consistent success with IBM, Art decided to take on a new challenge. A major financial institution was selling money management services to corporations. Many bankers, while friendly and service-oriented, are often noncompetitive. The institution decided that Art was the ideal person, as director of marketing, to help create a culture that would enable the bank's staff to sell their computer services.

Art was anxious to achieve the desired objectives, though his aggressiveness threatened people within the bank and upset certain personalities. Unknowingly, he was creating a conflict with those who were reluctant to change. After two years and seven months he was fired. He remembers that day:

I drove home that sunny October afternoon, realizing that exactly twenty seven years had passed since the day I had caused my team to lose. In my anxiousness to succeed I had again overthrown the ball. For a few days I felt disappointed. I had made a great effort to succeed, and instead I felt unappreciated and rejected. I had three children, two of them in college. My responsibility made me feel as though I had the weight of the world on my shoulders. Yet I kept my spirits up by reminding myself that, while I may have lost, I was not beaten. I was convinced I was still a winner, and I would soon be back on my feet. If I could keep that attitude, then it was only a matter of time before I would have a better job, and next time I would do better. Besides, the only way to really feel the high of winning is to have felt the disappointment of losing. A few months later I was re-hired by the same company to market a computer system to smaller banks who cannot afford the same technology, and I am now the national sales director.

> Our success begins with our expectations, is influenced by our perceptions and is determined by our reactions.

The more we expect of ourselves, the greater will be our determination to succeed. Yet our desire to win may cause us to be unable to tolerate failure. The solution is to reevaluate our expectations of reality and decide that our success requires failing frequently. If we cannot change what we expect of reality, then we need to change our perceptions. We could decide that what we had perceived to be failure was actually preparing us for greater success. If we are unable to change our expectations and perceptions, we can at least change our reactions.

This is the success that Art Mitchell created for himself. He expected to be a winner, regardless of whether or not he succeeded immediately. When he lost or was fired, he still did not perceive himself as a loser. He kept reacting as a winner. The consistency of his reactions, regardless of what was actually happening, eventually assured his victory.

Our reactions determine our feelings.

There is the true story of two sisters, one an alcoholic and one who never drank. Their father was an alcoholic, and both were asked the same question: "Why have you become the way you are?" Each gave the same explanation: "What can you expect when your father is an alcoholic?" Thus we are reminded that we are not a product of our environment, as important as the environment might be, but a product of our reactions to the environment. If we change our reactions, we can change the way we feel. If we are unable to change our reactions, then we need to change our perceptions.

If, ever again, we believe we have problems and feel frustrated, then we can change our perception by reading our daily newspaper. By page three we will most likely read an article about someone in so much trouble that, if we could swap problems, we would gladly take ours back. Most of us have never had a bad day in our lives, and if we think we have, then we need to reevaluate our perceptions of reality, of how difficult life can be.

Merely by changing our perceptions of what happened, we can change our reactions and, therefore, the way we feel. If we cannot change our perception of what occurred, then we have one last chance, which is to reevaluate our expectations. In review, we have a choice. By changing our expectations, perceptions or reactions we can change our feelings, our performance and our results.

Michael Blake suffered through poverty while writing screenplays that for years were never accepted. He admits, "I slept on a lot of floors," as friends would let him stay at their homes. Then he was diagnosed with Hodgkin's disease, a cancer of the lymph system, which is currently in remission.

Then he wrote a book that sold 30,000 copies. Kevin Costner liked the book and made the movie *Dances with Wolves*. Now the book has sold over 2 million copies, and Michael has won the Oscar for the movie adaptation.

He now enjoys speaking in schools and to homeless children. "I tell them that if you stay committed, your dreams can come true. I'm living proof of it. I left home at seventeen and had nothing but rejection for twenty-five years. I wrote more than twenty screenplays, but I never gave up."

Follow intuition and take action.

Our expectations influence our perceptions of reality, which determine our rate of success.

Our expectations create the intensity of our determination.

We balance confidence from success with humility from failure.

Failure makes us more aware of the difficulty within the opportunity.

Rather than being overwhelmed by a difficult environment, we keep reacting like winners.

12
A Chance to Grow

> We become our own heroes.

We may discover that the goal we are struggling to achieve is actually a futile effort. We might decide to channel our efforts towards aspirations that are more than just meaningful but also offer us a more reasonable chance of success. Once we have succeeded, we can reevaluate our expectations and decide if we want to seek the next plateau.

Developing Resiliency

At the age of seven Walter was alone in his backyard when he saw an owl asleep in a low-hanging branch. Intrigued by the idea of having his own friend, he quietly moved under the branch, then jumped and caught the owl by the claws. The owl, now awake, began tearing at his arm with its beak. In pain and fear, the boy slammed the owl to the ground and killed it. Then, with tears and guilt, he buried the owl, thinking to himself, "What can I do to make animals come alive, rather than what I've done, and make people feel happy, rather than sad?"

Walt Disney then spent his life making animals come alive to make people happy. The past is not important, but only our willingness to let our disappointments enhance our creativity.

Realizing Our Choices

A divorce or a business failure can cause us to become weaker or more resilient. *The choice is always ours.* Too often we make such decisions subconsciously and select a negative reaction, causing anxiety leading to depression. The next time we become disappointed, we need to make decisions that help us become more resilient. Our resiliency needs to be balanced with humility. Our strength should not harden us, but allow us to be more gentle.

Failure leads to maturity.

We want to appreciate how adversity makes us more aware of what we must confront. Negative experiences are not upsetting when we anticipate them as a normal part of the process of succeeding. If ever again we are disappointed, we must decide that we are now more familiar with how difficult this world can be.

The reason an experience upsets us is when it is less than what we expected. It is as though the experience is taking on a life of its own and speaks to us, saying, "And you thought, just by being charming, you were going to succeed. Obviously, you are not as mature as you thought you were. This challenge is going to require a little more pain and suffering than you were planning on. Don't take it personally and become disappointed, depressed, and defensive and decide to drop out. *You deserve the success.* You just have to experience a little more frustration and anxiety before you bridge the gap."

Traumatic changes in our life-style can force us to make decisions that assure our success.

Jeff Durkee is both self-reliant and receptive to new ideas. I asked Jeff if success came easily for him. He told me the following story:

> When I was thirteen, we were living in a wealthy neighborhood and enjoying all the benefits of luxury. Then my parents got divorced. We went from a membership in the country club to a membership in the food stamp club and living in a trailer.
> I had always been a likable kid. I was the class clown. Suddenly life was no longer an amusement. I was learning rapidly that I needed to take money seriously and be smart about financial mat-

ters. Whatever would happen would be up to me. I also knew that I wanted to go back to the affluence that I had experienced. The loss of what I had taken for granted had a profound impact on the direction of my life.

As I listened to Jeff I thought about people who are experiencing culture shock because of economic adversity. Possibly our ability to capitalize on difficult times is based on experiencing difficulty at an early age. Maybe that is why success did not come easily for me. I was sheltered in childhood: my mother loved me, and my father took care of me. I had no bad experiences and was unprepared for the challenge of adulthood.

After Jeff finished college, he applied to a major stockbrokerage firm. While many people told him he was too young for the job, he knew that he had matured beyond his years. He was hired and soon got his first big order. He recounted the experience:

> In my exuberance I made an error in the way I wrote the order and was severely criticized. It was a cold day in Atlanta, and I was feeling very rejected. I decided to walk the streets and began knocking on doors. I felt that getting out of the office when discouraged would help me do better. I visited a union, and the executive told me that he had a $100,000 check that he needed to deposit in a money market fund and asked if I could take care of him. Every year he placed the same order. Because of this incident, from that day, whenever I felt discouraged, I would knock on doors and see people.

The Heroic Journey

Jeff continued his story:

> Some of the lessons of life are difficult when you are going through them, but they make you a more complete person. I was naive of the fact that people do bad things and sometimes are not loving and nurturing. Rather than becoming bitter we need to take the heroic journey. I try to be a prince regardless of whether I am meeting dragons or swans. Once in a while I find a sage to help me along the way.

> | Be patient. |
> | --- |

Whenever I find myself having difficulty, I imagine that I am in a raft, traveling down a river. There is a turn in the bend, and I cannot see where I am going. I feel the excitement of the unexpected, and sometimes there is disaster. It is difficult when you are in a storm and wonder if you will ever enjoy yourself again. Yet the struggle helps you decide where you want to be.

> **Tragic times help us develop our resourcefulness.**

One of the purposes of life is to grow. *If you never experienced difficulty you may never discover how resourceful you can be.* You need to test your thought process to sharpen the way you think. You need to develop your judgment and problem-solving ability. Afterwards you are actually thankful that you had those opportunities that you would otherwise have referred to as tragedies.

> **Accept what we cannot change.**

Sometimes, though, the tragedy is too great to be explained philosophically. My wife and I recently lost our first child. Sometimes there is no explanation. The events of life appear often to be the result of random fate. It is easy to be optimistic and enthusiastic when all is going well and you can see victory at the next dawn. It is easy to fight when you know you can win. The challenge is to have the will to continue when it appears all is against you, when losing someone you loved or someone's approval. The key is to switch the thoughts in your mind and decide "I'm going to continue the struggle and the hero's journey, even if it appears there's no chance I'll succeed."

Jeff is now a branch manager for the same firm in the southwest. Though some may have thought that, at the age of twenty-nine, he was too young for the job, he has weathered a few storms and his results prove he is managing successfully.

There is solace in books that help us grow, but most of all we need to develop our own agenda. My next objective is to become my own coach and counselor while still benefiting from people who can help me along the way. My plan is to read one less book and devote the energy to developing my own unique thoughts as part of my own evolving.

When Jeff was thirteen and his father left, he had to be his own father. Now that he is the father of a new baby, he can be a child, growing again. We need to be mature when we are young and young when we are mature.

As I listened to Jeff, I thought of how, as we reach crossroads, we have choices. If we do what feels natural, we are reinforcing our usual patterns of thinking and behavior. What might be most needed is *doing what feels uncomfortable.* Only then do we break through our predictable patterns and reach new levels of performance and reward.

> Sometimes our failures and successes are only based on fate.

> We refuse to allow failure to damage our self-image.

> We decide that painful experiences actually establish new resiliencies that resolve old feelings of inadequacy.

13
Take
Risks

We gather our courage to take the first step and open ourselves to unpredictable adventure.

Factors for Success

Consider those qualities that make us more sophisticated than other animals, as well as more competitively successful among people. A basic factor is our dexterity. Our hands allow us to operate machines and capitalize on technology. People who are mechanically inclined often earn a good income.

Also important is our ability to communicate. The most famous people are often movie stars, religious leaders and political figures. Their charismatic style and ability to perform create their popularity and fame.

Generally, though, our intelligence is believed to be the primary factor. Great thinkers such as philosophers and professors attain positions of prestige. We revere great minds such as Socrates, Plato, Aristotle and Einstein.

Few people realize that, more important than our dexterity, ability to communicate and our intelligence is the fact that we are the only animal that is *risk-oriented*. All animals are territorial. Even monkeys and chimpanzees will become nervous if they venture beyond the invisible boundaries of their own territories. Of course there are some animals that are migratory, but while they often travel thousands of miles, they keep moving in an exact direction to a very specific place.

Only we, as explorers, pioneers and astronauts, seem fascinated with the idea of going beyond our boundaries. Though knowing we might confront danger, we are exhilarated with the thought of discovering how far we can go and how much we can accomplish.

Being risk-oriented can be unreasonably dangerous. We want to forecast the difficulty and reduce the possibility of experiencing significant loss. We also want to increase the odds of succeeding by understanding our strengths and liabilities. Then we determine the path that gives us the greatest opportunity of reaching our objective.

Regardless of how prepared we might be, there is always risk involved when exploring beyond our familiar environment. When the journey is unpredictable, we expose ourselves to varying degrees of disaster. Just the thought of losing what we already have might immobilize us. In that moment of hesitation there might be only one quality that will assure our success and that is our *courage to fail.* We take the first step and begin the adventure. We thrive on the exhilaration and *allow the anxiety to increase our momentum.*

Enjoying the Adventure

Today Heidi Trieschmann is the director of marketing for Pencor, a publishing and consulting company that helps accounting firms become more marketing-oriented. She teaches accountants how to develop strategies and techniques that can expand their business. Her ability to help other people become more successful has evolved through her own personal and business challenges. Her philosophy begins with the following belief:

> Everything happens for a reason. When someone is in trouble, help them, listen and try to understand how they cope and survive. By hearing what other people go through, you can learn about yourself and the way you deal with your problems and appreciate your situation better.
>
> Then there are times when you can't worry about everyone else. Sometimes you need time for yourself, such as being adventuresome in a totally different way. I will go backpacking or take a skiing trip. Once I took a fourteen-week survival course.
>
> I was in below-zero weather, and I quickly learned that you have to appreciate what you have. There were moments in which I felt I could not continue. I kept thinking, "I want my warm bed," but I had

no choice. I felt so cold. I would try to comfort myself that at least it was not snowing. Then it would snow, so I would try to feel better by telling myself at least it was not windy. Then it would get windy. After awhile it became humorous, and I tried not to think, "It could be worse" for fear of what would happen.

Appreciate the stress.

Whenever I am in a business challenge I think of how it could be worse. I appreciate the stress rather than feel sorry for myself. Thinking of something worse seems to keep me in balance when I'm in a storm. This is just one way of releasing my ego. When you let your ego get in the way, you often go in the wrong direction. When you release your ego, you can see much more clearly. You need your ego to feel the excitement of the adventure and your subconscious mind to keep you sensible in your decisions and direction.

Understand the choices.

You need to view survival as an adventure. Whether in the wilderness or in business the strategies and the choices are very similar. There are also some major differences. In business challenges you know you are not going to die, and you also have more choices and options in business. Mother Nature is often neither kind nor forgiving. In business you can seek people who, just as in a survival course, understand that working together can assure your success while making the journey easier.

Those of us who take the adventurous path will discover there are various ways to feel stimulated and excited. Unfortunately, some of us seek self-destructive addictions to feel alive, such as drugs or gambling. Some of us may even become addicted to dangerous sports such as hang gliding or motorcycle racing. If we fill our lives with purpose, we run the risk of disappointment. The solution is to formulate survival and success strategies.

The Courage to Do Battle

Heidi spoke about taking courage:

When caught in an ocean riptide, you don't fight it. Otherwise you may panic, exhaust yourself, get pulled under and die. When you are in a snowstorm, you make a shelter and wait it out. If you are not prepared for the challenge, then you cannot force the situation. However, you never can be perfectly prepared in business when so much of what you need to know comes only from the experience. There comes the moment when you gather your courage, take the first step, create the momentum and extend yourself 100 percent.

Know when to say it wasn't meant to be and when to do battle. Even when it was not meant to be, you can learn from it, but you never let go of those challenges that are important until you have conquered them.

Dangerous Opportunities

There are two characters in the Chinese language that represent the word *crisis*. One is the picture for danger; and the other, for opportunity. Therefore, we want to live life by seeking opportunities while minimizing the danger.

The idea is to increase the opportunity of succeeding while reducing the risk of danger. Some of us enjoy running precariously along the edge of possible disaster. The greater the risk, the more we feel alive. Realize that the safer path might reduce the danger, but also reduce the opportunity. The challenge is to take chances and capitalize on whatever happens. If we do experience difficult times, we then remember those people who suffered through greater challenges and, more than just surviving, succeeded.

Keeping Our Perceptions in Balance

Sometimes we become too aware of our own problems and forget that other people are experiencing more difficulty. One way that I keep my perceptions in balance is by reading books like *Touching the Void* by Joe Simpson.

Joe and his companion, Simon, had just climbed a 20,000-foot mountain in the Andes. Having only descended 1000 feet, Joe fell. When he landed, the impact was so great that it drove his left leg through his knee, shattering his leg in five major areas.

Simon now began lowering Joe down the mountain with a rope, 150 feet at a time. A blizzard hit that was so severe that Simon could not see or hear Joe beyond fifty feet. Unknowingly, he lowered Joe off the edge of a cliff. He knew the moment that Joe went over the edge by the reaction of the rope.

Simon continued to lower Joe the entire 150 feet, but Joe was still hanging helplessly in the storm. Simon physically could not lift Joe back up, and Joe could not take care of himself. Simon had only one option. He cut the rope and hoped, with Joe's shattered leg, that the fall was not too great. Simon then worked his way down, looking for the point where Joe had fallen, only to discover that Joe had disappeared into a deep crevice in the earth. Simon assumed that Joe could not have lived through such a fall. He returned to the camp, unaware that Joe had safely landed on a ledge within the crevice.

Securing the rope to a piton that he quickly hammered into the ice wall, Joe then spent a horrible night in the crevice, hungry, very cold, and in severe pain from his shattered leg.

The next morning, at the first light of dawn, Joe realized his situation. He could not get up the ice wall, but the other side showed some possibilities. He lowered himself to the bottom of the crevice, dragged himself to the other side and then, piton by piton, reached the top by sunset. It took Joe three days to crawl six miles, every movement causing extreme pain. Hungry and frostbitten, he finally reached camp and safety.

These are the kinds of books that we need to read when we think we are having a bad day. They change our perception of reality and remind us of how much more difficult this world can be. We need to find a moment each day to *balance our perceptions of reality.* While we want to be cognizant of the crisis before it occurs, we do not have to worry about the myriad petty problems that may never happen. *Balance is the answer.*

Many years ago I showed a motivational movie on my lecture tour about Harry Cordellos, who is blind. The film shows him running a seven-mile race north of San Francisco, up steps, through a redwood forest, across a meadow and down a rocky trail, holding onto his friend's arm who guided him the entire distance.

When the film was finished, rather than comment on the movie, I would discuss the Culver City marathon, which I ran in 1977. I had made the turn at the halfway mark and, with thirteen miles to go, saw Dr. Peter Strudwick moving toward me, running in last place. Peter was born without feet or hands. He runs on the stubs of his legs. As Peter approached me, I decided to say nothing to him, as I thought any comment might be inappropriate. Yet, as he passed me, he encouraged me, "You're looking good; keep it up."

More recently, Harry Cordellos ran a long-distance race while holding on to Peter Strudwick's arm. If ever we think we are having a bad day, we need to remember Harry, blind, and Peter, running on the stubs of his legs, both hanging onto each other for so many miles, and ask ourselves, "How can I ever again claim to have a bad day?"

Today Dr. Peter Strudwick, with a graduate degree in psychology, gives lectures on tenacity, imagination and discipline. He believes that "when we are born we are dealt a hand of cards. We play the cards as best we can, but there are no handicaps." We never allow obstacles to prevent us from moving toward our objectives.

Creating a Positive Cycle

I always enjoy watching reruns of the Carol Burnett show. Carol was raised by her grandmother. They lived on welfare. She attributes her survival and success to her ignorance of the odds against her. As she said in an article by Eric Sherman in *Ladies' Home Journal*, "I didn't know I couldn't get out of being poor when I was a kid. Who would have thought I could be in show business? Nobody but me. I think it's important to take risks, to risk defeat. And to find out you can live through one or two or three or more."

Some of us think too much of all the reasons why we might fail. Such thinking does not prepare us for the challenge. Rather our fears are convincing us to avoid the effort. Better instead that we ignore our fears and pursue our goals, as though we were a mule with blinders along a canyon path. Otherwise we will be immobilized by the sheer drop beyond the edge.

> Pack away our fears and master the opportunities.

We can make our life as we wish it to be. We can become entrepreneurial and work at home, rather than fight freeway traffic. We can master computer technology and have all the information we need instantly to take greater control of our lives. We can work more on weekends when the city is silent and have our days off during the week when the beach and mountain resorts are quiet.

As children we often are inhibited by our insecurities. Adults are so much bigger, stronger and more intelligent. An older child can run faster and a parent can win most any argument because of their ability to use logic, even when we know we are right. Then the years pass by and, while we may become stronger and better educated, too often we still may feel unsure of ourselves. Our inadequacies, rather than being packed away in the attic with our toys of childhood, too often stay with us. Our fears speak to us and take away our desire to try. They frighten us until we lose our courage. We need to accept our feelings of inadequacy as a natural part of our childhood. Then we should pack them away and reach out for what we want.

> Take control by creating positive cycles.

Failure and rejection, when taken personally, can cause ego damage and depression. We need to disengage from this negative process and *create a positive cycle*. We want to create success, receive positive feedback, increase our self-esteem and feel good. Changing our attitude toward failure and rejection can strengthen our ego. Our objective is not to control people nor live their lives. Rather we want to be in control of our own lives.

Joan Lunden, a cohost of "Good Morning America," was thirteen when her father, a doctor, was killed in a private plane crash. She told Tom Seligson in *Parade* magazine, "Until then, I'd had a pretty comfortable life, but all of a sudden the bottom dropped out and my security was gone. With two kids, my mother really had to struggle. That's when I first decided I would always rely on my own strength and be in control of my own life."

Our ability to communicate effectively and our intelligence are two qualities primary to our success. Even more important are our courage, adventuresome spirit and desire to take chances.

Reacting Regardless of Risk

Thomas Keneally wrote a book about the true and heroic story of Oscar Schindler entitled *Schindler's List*. Oscar, during World War II, owned a work camp of Jews whom he protected. In another slave camp, in which the Jews were taken outside of the fence to work, one of the prisoners swapped a tool for a chicken with a farmer. When he realized he would be searched, he left the chicken outside the camp.

When the chicken was found by a guard, the Jews were lined up and asked, "Whose chicken is this?" No one answered, so a prisoner was shot, the bullet ripping through his head and killing the man next to him. The Jews were asked again, "Whose chicken?" and a boy of 14, stepping out of line and in tears, said he knew.

The commandant asked, "Who then?" and the boy pointed to one of the dead men. The commandant laughed. The incident was over.

Often, when we find ourselves in a conflict, we can think, deliberate and worry about the outcome or follow our intuition and take action. Sometimes we have no time to think, but do whatever comes to mind.

Be courageous and risk-oriented.

Being exhilarated by anxiety can assure our momentum.

There are no bad days when we keep our perceptions in balance with reality.

We disregard our distractions and pursue our goals.

We pack away our fears and reach out for what we deserve.

We have the courage to explore beyond our boundaries.

14
Managing Our Feelings

Enthusiasm and anxiety can fuse into
a single force of positive energy.

Rivers of Emotions

Our results, such as how much money we earn, are by-products of how we behave, and we behave according to how we feel. Within each of us flow two rivers of emotions. One river is labeled *enthusiasm*. When we feel psyched, our behavior will usually be courageous and risk-oriented. The results, if we remain consistent, will be significant.

Yet, even within the most optimistic of us, exists a river of negative feelings. We refer to the states these emotions bring about as *depression, despair* or *moodiness*. When these melancholy feelings take over, our behavior usually is cautious, protective and defensive. The results of our work, at best, are usually minimal.

Our challenge is to control the river of our own feelings.

Talking to Ourselves

Currently, Stephen Peckham teaches people how to develop their potential. The only major trauma that Stephen ever experienced was when his wife divorced him. He found himself living in a tiny room and working three jobs to take care of his financial responsibilities. One of these jobs was part-time in a mental hospital. Helping people who were experiencing mental illness because of their inability to deal with reality helped Stephen to persevere through his own troubles.

One fascinating concept is "self-talk." People who are mentally ill talk to themselves, but so do those who are successful. *The secret of success is what we say to ourselves.* If we tell ourselves we are going to succeed and we fail, we might not want to try again. If we tell ourselves that we should seek only the safe path, we might become more protective and less productive. We want to tell ourselves that, regardless of what happens, we deserve to succeed. If we keep experimenting and persevere, we will eventually reach our expectations.

While each of us can have the same experience, our thoughts, feelings and reactions to that experience may be very different. Our thoughts, rather than being positive or negative, must be realistic. For example, some of us may decide, negatively, that a new experience is dangerous since we might fail and lose what we have already gained. Others of us might view, positively, the same experience as an opportunity to break out of the boredom of our predictable patterns. In reality, if the challenge were starting a new business and there were reasons why we might fail, then negative thinking is realistic.

Even more important, some of us may see reality for exactly what it is, while others of us see *reality for what it can become.* There are those of us who are fatalistic and believe that we have little opportunity to change the direction of our lives, while others of us feel confident that we can influence our future. The way we talk to ourselves can determine whether we fail or succeed. Our conversation needs to be realistic, not based on reality as it is, but on reality as we want it to be. Stephen explained his approach:

> I now know that when I hit a wall is when I learn the most. I have *learned more from my failures than my successes.* Real growth comes from always asking myself what is good about any failure. Just imagine yourself as being blind and alone in a room. You want to find the open door. Running into the wall is not a reason to give up. Hitting the wall should merely encourage us to keep reaching out and turning in new directions until we find our way. In this world of instant results it is still helpful to slow down and carefully feel our way through a problem.

More than one a single great effort, our success depends on the consistency of our effort. The objective is not to avoid failure but to *know what we need to fail at more frequently.* In selling, if we double our attempts in high-payoff activities, though we may double our failures, we will usually double our income. This formula applies with most opportunities.

We each need to allow ourselves a period of time to fail. You can *always grow from failure.* I admit, though, that rejection was much harder to overcome, maybe because of my divorce. The solution again was my self-talk. Once I programmed myself to understand that business contacts are not rejecting me personally, then the stress stays at a workable level. Otherwise you start losing control.

As a child Stevie was told by one of his teachers that he had three strikes against him. He was black, poor and blind. He would only be able to make rugs and pot holders. By the time he was twelve, he was acknowledged as a genius. Stevie Wonder explained in a *Radio Times* interview with Mike Brown, "You go through things that are relatively insignificant and pick out the ones that are important. The people I feel sorry for are those who have sight but still don't see." (Mick Brown Radio Times, England)

By *allowing adversity to sharpen our objectivity,* we can change the way we think. Just one thought can change our attitude toward failure, our perceptions of reality, our expectations of ourselves and therefore our reactions and results.

> **We can control the river of our feelings.**

> **Reality is based on our ability to fulfill our expectations.**

15
Finding Adventure

New experiences help us break out of
our old, predictable patterns.

The God of Chaos

In the Hindu religion there are three gods. The first is Brahma, the creator of all that exists. The second is Vishnu, the preserver and protector of all that Brahma has created. The third is Shiva, the god of chaos and destruction. In this religion Shiva is a positive force, for only in death can we begin the creative cycle. Like the phoenix, which is reborn from the ashes, we can also renew ourselves.

Life is not always to be viewed as a straight line, one day following another, but as a cycle, as in the passing of the seasons. Think of a walk in the forest on a cold winter day when the sun offers little comfort. The landscape is white and brown, patches of snow and earth. There are no green leaves or grass, and the trees appear dead and lifeless. Yet in the first warmth of springtime the earth will come alive, the trees will appear stronger and taller—symbolic of life evolving and perfecting.

We want to be children again, feeling the excitement of a new adventure. Every time we take on a new challenge, we are entering a passageway. We are usually unable to predict the conclusion or even what we may experience along the way. Yet, when our journey is completed and we look back with satisfaction at what we have accomplished, we have also *positioned ourselves to begin the cycle again.*

Just as children feel frightened when leaving home to go to school for the first time, we may feel insecure leaving home to begin our lives as adults. We enter a new passageway, often feeling apprehensive but also exhilarated by our self-sufficiency. Passageways are places of mixed emotions. We feel anxious that we might fail while exhilarated by the opportunities to succeed.

We can imagine life as a spiraling staircase, moving ever upward. If we ever feel overwhelmed, we can stop and catch our breath. When we experience success, we can pause, as though on a platform, to enjoy the satisfaction of what we have accomplished.

Soon we may feel comfortable, as our success becomes an automatic routine. Gradually, we may develop conflicting emotions: We are comfortable staying where we are, yet restless to take on the next challenge. If we stay where we are, we might feel safe and secure but be in danger of depression from boredom. Security is also an illusion if we think the safe path will protect us from the unpredictableness of life.

Predictable Patterns

True security occurs when we prepare ourselves for the challenges before they occur. The adventurous road might take us into unexpected places. However, if we make the trip with frequency, we will soon discover that there are certain predictable patterns to this path.

First we can predict that we will feel apprehension. This emotion can range between being really frightened to merely worried. Why do we worry so often and so easily? Maybe it is a built-in device to assure our survival. If we did not worry, then we might not recognize our problems until it was too late. Yet we need to worry productively. What we worry about should get us ready for reality and not cause us to self-destruct.

So often we worry needlessly. This may be a survival reaction from primitive times. Mark Twain has been credited with saying, "Half of what I ever worried about never happened." For many of us, almost all we worry about never occurs.

We need to manage the way we worry so that we only become upset in ways that increase our success. If we feel pain, we need to worry so that if we have a medical problem we can catch it before it is too late. If we want to achieve an important objective, we can create a sense of urgency which prepares us for the challenge. If we feel particularly nervous about making an error, then we can take cautious steps.

Once I was teaching my older son to catch a football. I would throw the ball to him, but he consistently fumbled it. I knew he was frustrated, and the experience was not helping his self-image. Then I left on a week's lecture trip.

When I returned, we tried again, and he did very well. I asked his mother if there was any reason for his dramatic improvement. She said they had been practicing by her handing the ball to him then taking one step back and tossing it only a couple of feet and, as he gained confidence, gradually taking more steps back and thereby comfortably increasing the distance.

As we pursue our objective, we develop patterns of success that become stratas of strength within our self-image. Gradually we develop the confidence that whenever we experience adversity, we will have these patterns to fall back on.

Seeking Satisfaction through Success

I met Mike Forster in 1973 in New Orleans while I was giving a lecture for IBM management. Mike was with IBM for twenty-four years. At one time his dream was to be an IBM manager, and when he had achieved that objective, he set new goals. When he reached the level of vice president, he realized that his success had taken him away from the activities he enjoyed.

In 1992 Mike introduced me to over 1000 Computervision people for their annual international convention. Afterwards Mike told me the following:

> Self-analysis has to be the first strength. I need to understand what I enjoy. If I am devoting a major part of my life to work, then I want *the challenge to be fun.*
>
> At one point in my life an opportunity came to leave IBM and do what I find most satisfying. Yet it was incredible to actually think of leaving the womb of IBM with all the security and sense of protection, but the request was made from someone I respected.

> We often take the path that runs along the edge.

A basic truth is that we have choices. If we are locked into one path, we often deny ourselves the vision to recognize all the opportunities. Yet within a short time after leaving IBM I felt I had gone from the proverbial frying pan into the fire. My new company was attacked in a hostile takeover and, to save itself, went into a leverage buyout that created a one-billion-dollar debt. The person who hired me left the company, and we went through three CEOs. I felt I was running along a precipice.

Every time I felt as though the problems were serious, I would return to a few basic truths. First, make sure that you are enjoying the trip. Second, whatever happens is an opportunity for growth. Finally, regardless of how difficult the circumstances, know that you are building an experience that will make you stronger, more resilient and flexible.

> **Develop potential by moving through the frustrations.**

If you focus on the objectives you wish to achieve, then the frustrations often disappear. Change requires taking on challenges replete with frustrations. I know I'll make mistakes but I will have no one to blame but myself. How much easier to decide to move on to self-fulfillment.

> **By breaking out of our comfort zone, we expand the arena of our opportunities.**

I know that if I stay committed to my values, such as staying focused on the customers, I will strengthen my foundation. Also, knowing your strengths and weaknesses can give you an incredible calm. As I move into the future, I know my comfort zone as well as *the areas in which I need to test myself.* I imagine that I am on a playing field and within the arena are areas in which I feel secure. Widening the arena to expand the opportunities to win the game becomes the challenge. If I become too comfortable, I can easily become negative and want to give up when frustrated. Then the fundamentals strengthen my resolve as I remember what I have learned and realize the value of what I have experienced.

Mike is now the European manager for Computervision. His ability to be objective when solving his own problems has kept him on target.

The Value of Transformation

> **There is always a trade-off.**

Failure can take many forms. For example, in February of 1990 I was a month away from reaching the age of fifty and looking forward to competing in a new age group in long-distance running. When I was forty five, I had qualified for the World Games in Rome for the Senior Olympics by running 10 kilometers (6.2 miles) in 34 minutes, 26 seconds, an average of 5 minutes, 32 seconds per mile. Now I wanted to see how good I could be at fifty. But, on preparing to board an airplane, I picked up my luggage and damaged a muscle in my left hip. For the first time in twenty years I had to stop running.

There were times when I would be lecturing and hear myself discussing the idea that, in most every failure, there is a trade-off. Frustrated that I could not run, I decided to transfer the energy I expended in running to cycling and swimming, which did not irritate my injury. Even then, these physical activities were not satisfying enough to compensate for my addiction to running, so I decided to write a book.

Whatever benefits you might gain from these ideas, as well as my own satisfaction in completing this manuscript, would not have been possible if I had not replaced a frustration with an accomplishment.

So often we feel secure by staying with our own patterns, such as our job, watching our favorite television programs, or a love relationship. If we were to lose our job, the television were to break or the relationship end, we might feel more than insecure. We might feel as though we had lost the foundation of our life. We then determine the trade-off by deciding how we replace what we have lost.

The shock of a broken routine can stimulate us to explore our potential, experiment, and develop new areas of interest. If a relationship ends and we are heartbroken, then we need to channel our frustrations into reading poetry at sunset or renewing an old friendship. When we are frustrated by financial problems, we can convert a personal interest into a part-time job. We find the trade-off that compensates for our loss. Even though the loss is beyond our control, we can still create new experiences that add value to our lives. Then the failure works for our benefit.

My loss of running has allowed me to enjoy cycling through forests, snorkeling in the ocean and pursuing the challenge of writing a new book. We all need to understand *the value of transformation in our lives.*

> **We sift through the ashes of our loss to find significance in our failures.**

Tony Friend was with IBM in 1978 when he coordinated a series of lectures I was giving in Sydney, Australia. A few years ago, he was crippled by an unidentifiable disease that left him with a spastic walk. It took three years of constant testing to isolate the problem as a rare, incurable neurological disease. Tony will never again be able to enjoy his passion for skiing and ocean sailing. He is also honest about his emotions:

> For four months I was very depressed. The final diagnosis, with the stark realization that this problem would never go away, occurred when my business was down, which then hurt my marriage. My optimism, which had always saved me, was not equal to the feelings of despair. I would dig down within myself but could not find enough strength. I had to dig very deep to find the strength to keep going. I believe you can always dig down deeper until you come to terms with your fate. You have to drag yourself up by deciding never to give up.
>
> I kept asking myself, "When do you give up on persistence?" You have to believe that when one door closes another one opens. If you keep making intelligent decisions, you can separate your mind from your emotions. The objectivity of your thoughts can then protect you from the feelings that might otherwise bring you down.

> **Find strength in the memories of past successes.**

> Fifteen years before, I had been selling for IBM, and I couldn't see any way of making quota, nor could I see anything on the horizon that would save me. Then I convinced myself that the environment is always changing. Just because the day is bleak is no reason to believe tomorrow will be the same. If the environment is always changing, then you have to recognize the coming of new opportunities. A change in IBM's marketing strategy presented me with an opportunity, which I grasped enthusiastically. Suddenly, one morning, I visualized exactly how this change would impact my customers. That same morning I made three presentations and made my quota. You never give up.

Then Tony thought of his seventy-eight-year-old father who, when seventy, had a heart attack and almost died. At first his situation seemed so serious that Tony's mother was told by the doctors he would not survive and she might as well take home his clothing. When he recovered, she brought back his clothes. What could she say when he asked her why she had taken his clothes home? When Tony's father returned home, he had become bitter and unpleasant. Tony explained it this way:

He struggled to be positive but could not seem to make the transition back to a normal life. Then he found a new lease on life. At seventy-six he bought a computer and fell in love with the challenge of learning and enjoying all he could do with it. Now he walks five miles per day and reminds us that you are never too old to take advantage of the opportunities you do have.

Tony is living in Tiburon, California, still in love and happily married, enjoying what he can do and devoting his energy to his business. He accepts what he cannot change and has the courage to confront what he can control. Recently he shared with me his grandfather's thoughts that have helped him to stay objective and persevere through his own adversity and depression:

To all the problems under the sun
there be a solution
or there be none.
If there be one,
try to find it;
if there be none,
never mind it.

Enjoy the journey.

We find strength in the memories of our past success.

We see reality for what it can become.

16
Becoming More Creative

> Failure develops our potential, enhances our self-image and increases our self-esteem.

Failure as Positive

We live in a society that believes winning is not the most important thing; winning is the only thing. Of course, winning is the best experience of all. Success is exciting and satisfying. Yet success might actually be dangerous. Success can lead to boredom and apathy.

As an example, George Sanders, a British actor, enjoyed wealth, fame, glory, recognition and financial independence. He also married beautiful women, including Zsa Zsa Gabor. When George achieved all his goals in life, he gave himself a promised gift: retirement to his lovely villa in Spain. Then he shot himself in the head. His suicide note was very brief: "The reason I decided to leave was because I have become so bored." It is unfortunate that people should ever become so successful and satisfied that they become bored and depressed.

Failure Becomes Our Friend

Children who are never given the opportunity to express their frustrations will often find indirect ways to release their tension. They might interrupt us when we are talking to someone or cry in the middle of the night and disturb our sleep. If, equally, we disregard the hurt feelings of our inner child, we will often be distracted by our repressed feelings. Listening to our unhappiness can release the negative feelings and help us move into the future. It is never too late to have a happy childhood.

If we disregard the negative experience that is upsetting us, then we are allowing failure to become our enemy. Soon the frustration may deepen until we have no idea why we are depressed. The solution is to make failure a good friend by finding a time each day to allow our frustrations to speak to us. By taking a walk at sunset or lighting a candle at midnight, we create a quiet place within our day. Then we can more easily hear our frustrations.

As we listen to our feelings, we allow our disappointment to be expressed. We can understand what is important to us, as well as our vulnerabilities. Afterwards we can decide how the experience will help us to mature and become more resilient.

Consider how objective we can be for the benefit of others. We can often see our problems clearly and form great solutions, whether or not we express our understanding. Now consider why we might lose objectivity for our own benefit. The problem is we take ourselves too seriously. The solution is to realize that when we express our frustrations, 80 percent of the people don't even care, and 20 percent are glad! While that is not a pleasant story, it is equally unpleasant if we take ourselves so seriously and fear others' reactions so much as to cost us our own objectivity.

Think of the tension we often feel in the morning in our lower back muscles, which by early afternoon has reached our shoulders and by late in the day has caused our head to ache. The pain is caused by anxiety, tension and stress. When these toxic forms of energy graduate beyond a certain level, we may find ourselves losing objectivity and becoming either depressed or irritable.

There is a solution. Before allowing anxiety to graduate to this level, we need to do the following:

Stop what we are doing.

Step outside ourselves.

Look back at what occurred.

Change our perception of what happened.

When we change our perception of reality, we are forcing reality to separate, until it splits open and the tension spills out. Humor is the releasing of tension.

> **Humor is the distortion of reality.**

If we distort reality too much, people might say, "That wasn't funny. That was ridiculous!" If we do not distort reality enough, people may say, "That wasn't funny. That was too serious." Therefore, our responsibility is to catch ourselves before the anxiety causes us to lose objectivity. Then we stop what we are doing, look back at what occurred, and change our perception of what happened. In other words, we find the humor in our own frustration, and our tension is released.

A Sense of the Absurd

Mike Noiseaux has had his share of rejections but depends on humor, as practiced by his Irish ancestors, to keep himself going. Mike described this to me:

> The Irish have been through famine and poverty, but they face the challenge of life by keeping their sense of humor. If you can't laugh in the face of adversity, you are not going to press on. I've been through an extraordinarily painful divorce and a downturn in the economy that has hurt me financially. Yet every time I've taken a bad hit in the head, I've found a way to laugh at it. Turning a phrase to find a sense of the ridiculous can help us find a sense of the absurd in our lives.

The Passage of Time

We can all think of an experience that happened many years ago that was so embarrassing we did not want anyone to know about it. However, as the years passed, it became one of our favorite stories, to be told to friends at social gatherings and strangers in coffee shops. Consider what happened to cause the experience to go from being one of the most humiliating to one of the funniest of our life. What caused the transition? *Time.* In the passage of time it began to appear as though the experience happened to someone else. Therefore, when in a down cycle we need to speed up time.

Time travels at different speeds. When we feel depressed and time is painfully taking forever, we can increase the speed of time by following any combination of these solutions:

Make a war story out of this difficult experience by telling someone what occurred.

Listen to a tape cassette of a comedian we enjoy.

Change our perception of what happened.

In other words, we can find the humor in our own frailties and amusement in our own frustrations. In these ways we can more quickly pull ourselves out of a down cycle and get back on schedule.

> **Trauma becomes humorous when converted into a war story.**

As a personal illustration, my wife and I were in Rome recently. We had just purchased train tickets to Venice and Florence, and were walking up the steps to the Villa Borgia Park. In front of us were four gypsy girls. As we approached them, they stood up so we could pass.

As I walked by them, one girl began waving a newspaper in my face, as though trying to sell it to me. I was politely disregarding her when, from somewhere in my mind a voice said to me, "You just lost your wallet." I reached into my pocket and it was gone.

I was more than distressed as I turned to my wife and told her, "They have everything. All our credit cards, passports, plane tickets and money." I turned back to the girls and demanded my wallet back. They all ran. I grabbed the second oldest who appeared to be about eleven. She was my hostage. If the girls wanted her back, they would have to return my wallet. I dragged her down the steps into a piazza, yelling, "Dove un polizia." She then took all her clothing off to prove to me that she did not have the wallet. At that point there were fifty Italians wondering why I was holding onto this naked, struggling eleven-year-old girl. But I'm from New York, so this was no big deal to me.

She then fell to the ground, as though in a convulsion, with saliva coming out of her mouth. Now there were a hundred Italians wondering why I was holding onto this naked little girl. A few minutes later the three girls returned. We swapped the little girl for my wallet, and I said to my wife, "Tell no one. This has been too traumatic for me." Yet within three days, on trains and in restaurants, I was telling everyone what occurred.

> **Whatever frustrates us can also amuse us.**

We each can remember experiences that traumatized us and the frustration that the situation created. If we kept the anxiety within ourselves, the negative emotions often generated more emotional pressure, until we could no longer deal with any more tension. Then we found ourselves avoiding any challenges that might have caused further stress.

However, if we can find the humor in our frailties, then that which traumatizes us will amuse us. The tension is quickly released. Soon we may feel bored because there is no stress in our lives. Then the only solution is to take on a new challenge and renew the energy of our adventuresome spirit.

Curiosity and Adventure

Instinctive within our primitive nature is both an attraction and a fear of the unfamiliar. Our curiosity motivates us to explore beyond the horizon while being frightened that what we discover might be dangerous or destroy us.

We have so many culturally conditioned thoughts to persuade us to be adventurous and also cautious: "Curiosity killed the cat," *so be cautious*; "familiarity breeds contempt," *so staying in the same place causes us to hate what we have.*

Animals in a cage often show signs of stress. The people who manage the zoo need to understand what is causing the animals' stress in order to decide on the most appropriate solution. Some animals are frightened and need to feel more secure; other animals are bored. The zookeeper determines the cause of the frustration by placing a strange object in the cage. If the animal is curious and plays with the object, then the cause of its anxiety is boredom. If it seems frightened by the object, then it is probably feeling insecure.

If we apply this test to ourselves, we might better understand our frustrations. If change causes apprehension and our only desire is to stay in our present routine, then we are probably feeling insecure. Regardless of how cautious we might feel, we want to remember that deep within us is a child of curiosity who loves new challenges. If we enjoy change, then our frustrations can usually be resolved by taking on a new adventure.

If we lack ego resiliency, then even minor or petty situations may be upsetting. If we cannot change our attitude toward failure and we continue to experience anxiety, then we need to relieve ourselves of the tension before we become overwhelmed and give up.

Our humor becomes creative and disarming when we add humility.

Will Rogers, the famous humorist and philosopher, was about to meet President Coolidge. Coolidge was a very serious man of few words. He once gave a speech of just one word, "Good-bye." On another occasion a woman, upon meeting him, said, "I have a bet with a friend that I can get you to say at least three words," and he said, "You lose."

A friend bet Will that he could not get Calvin to laugh within twenty minutes after meeting him. Will accepted, and the introduction followed: "President Coolidge, Will Rogers. Will Rogers, President Coolidge." Will Rogers asked, "Excuse me, your name again?" He had won the bet in seven seconds.

When our world is not all we hoped it would be, then failure and rejection can cause anxiety. Keeping the anxiety inside of us may weigh us down, causing depression. Rather than allow the depression to deepen, we can instead find the humor in our own frailties. We speed up time by becoming amused with the person who had the bad experience, as though that person were someone else.

Comedians, to be successful, must find amusement in their own frustrations. Consider the humor of Rodney Dangerfield:

> I didn't feel good! I went to the doctor and he said I had a virus. I said, "I want a second opinion." He said, "You're ugly too!"
>
> And last month we had a fire in the house. My kids were yelling, "Fire, fire," and my wife's yelling, "Shut up! Dad's sleeping!" I'll tell ya. No respect!
>
> I sent my picture to a lonely hearts club. They mailed it back. They said, "We're not that lonely!"
>
> I said to my psychiatrist, "I got suicidal tendencies." Now he's billing me in advance.

What Rodney Dangerfield does for us is what we need to do for ourselves. We need to find humor in our own frailties and amusement in our frustrations.

Think of how failure helps us develop our potential. In other words, how does failure enhance our self-image? Recognize the positive relationship between failure and self-esteem. For most of us, there will come a day that is not all we hoped it would be. On that day, remember why *we need failure in our life to develop our potential, enhance our self-image, and gain self-esteem.*

Change our perception of reality and we release the tension.

We can find the humor in our own frailties.

We use our mind to create images of the way we want our life to be.

2

Rejection, Feedback That Strengthens Our Self-Image

17
Become Courageous

True security is in the strengths we create within ourselves.

Understanding Our Vulnerabilities

Rejection is usually a more negative experience than failure. For many of us failure would not be so upsetting if no one knew about it. The problem is not failing, but the humiliation that failure causes us.

Children who are learning to walk will stumble and fall, but the applause from their parents encourages them to continue. Today, if we stumble and fall, rather than being applauded, we will probably feel embarrassed. Even mispronouncing a word can cause us to feel foolish.

The fear of failure is not part of our nature. As children we are naturally curious. We love to explore and ask questions. Inherent within us is not the fear of failure but the fear of rejection. As long as we feel loved for who we are, we will feel encouraged to be adventurous and develop our talents.

Unfortunately, for most of us, a stage occurs within our development that inhibits us. At an early age we might experience rejection. People become irritated with our endless questions and curiosity. They may become impatient with us, and their negative feedback soon causes us to lose our curiosity. We can all remember the first time we attempted something new, such as riding a bike, with our parents cautioning, "Watch out, you might hurt yourself." We need to recognize the delicate balance between our awareness of danger and our desire to excel.

Soon, as children, we began to worry, not so much about making mistakes, but about being punished. Our natural exuberance and curiosity was repressed. Rather than being exploratory and risk-oriented, we became cautious and defensive.

Removing the Stigma of Defeat

We need to be children again, allowing ourselves the right to fail without the stigma of defeat and embarrassment. Yet we do not want to feel overwhelmed by constant change. How do we create the balance between feeling comfortable and taking chances?

The solution begins with an understanding of our values, of what is important to us. There is no need to learn how to repair a car or learn a foreign language if we have no need or interest in such skills. Rather we should focus our mind and efforts on those challenges that relate to our potential and values.

Focusing on a Positive Obsession

The route to success can be as simple as channeling all of our energy into a single positive obsession. There are two criteria that determine which objective to select. The first is financial reward. We deserve to enjoy affluence. The second is ego satisfaction. We want to enjoy our work. If we are devoting a major percentage of our life to our job, then we want to be sure that the challenge is at least as much fun as our favorite physical activity or watching a good movie.

If we are unable to find an occupation that is both financially rewarding and ego satisfying, then we need to separate our life into two parts. The first part involves the job that provides us with the money we desire, while the other involves the activity we enjoy. Ideally, the ego-satisfying activity might turn into a profitable venture. Then we can afford to do only what we enjoy.

Unfortunately, the more we want something, such as a relationship or success in business, the more fearful we might be of losing it. For this reason many of us avoid having expensive possessions such as luxury cars or jewelry, because we do not want to worry about objects that can be taken from us. Many of us also avoid challenges in our job, for the greater the responsibility, the greater the possible loss.

Rather than having a fear of success, we have a fear of the precarious position in which success places us. I have a fear of heights. The higher I hike along a High Sierra trail, the more exhilarated I become by the mountain landscapes and waterfalls. I also become more frightened as I look down and see how far I could fall. Similarly, in business, the greater the heights we reach, the more fearful we might become of how far we can fall.

Many of us believe that motivation is for people who are having difficulty succeeding. Yet the more successful we become, the more we have to lose. The possibility of embarrassment and stress also increases.

Think of the "Peter Principle," which explains that people rise to their level of incompetence. In other words, if we succeed in one job, we are usually promoted to the next level. As long as we are productive, we will continue to be promoted until we take on responsibilities that are beyond our ability. This increases the possibility that we will eventually fail.

If we are not ready for our next challenge, then we should avoid overextending ourselves. Otherwise we might self-destruct. This is not to say that we should compromise our aspirations. Rather we succeed by capitalizing on our existing strengths while "stretching ourselves" into our next challenge.

> **The higher we climb the ladder, the more magnified our misfortunes might become.**

If you are in selling and lose an order, no one knows you failed. If you succeed and are promoted into sales management and then one of your salespeople quits, everyone knows what happened. If the salesperson tells everyone in the office that you were the reason for his or her leaving, the exposure might be very negative.

If we were to run for political office in a small town and fail, the embarrassment might be confined to publicity in the local newspaper. When Richard Nixon had to resign as President, his defeat and humiliation was witnessed throughout the world.

The more we accomplish, the greater the opportunity to reach higher levels of success, but the more disastrous can be our downfall. There are three solutions:

- Break the challenge into incremental steps so that any failure we experience is minimized.

- Use rejection as a feedback device for self-improvement so that we understand how to improve the way we deal with people.

- Channel anxiety into a creative force for achievement so that when we are frustrated we become more productive.

The challenge is to *experience our vulnerabilities* and have the courage to grow through them until we have established new resiliencies.

Persevere Patiently

Abraham Lincoln's mother died in his childhood. The lady he loved and was engaged to marry also died. When his grocery business went bankrupt, he worked for seventeen years to pay back his creditors, although he was no longer obligated to do so. He tried politics and was defeated by the voters many times. He struggled to achieve noble aspirations and often was depressed by the struggle, but he persevered with dignity and patience.

If we persevere, without patience, we will probably succeed, but be frequently frustrated. If we are patient, without perseverance, we will probably be comfortable but never achieve our objectives. We want to keep ourselves in balance by having both qualities at the same time.

Cultural Conditioning

Our fears are often caused by cultural conditioning. We are taught that winning is not the most important thing—winning is the only thing. If you are being paid $3 million as a quarterback to win the Super Bowl, then having such an attitude might be crucial. Yet most of us need to find a balance between the demand to excel and enjoyment of the pursuit of excellence.

If we want to succeed, but we cannot deal with failure and rejection, we might not even try. If we do succeed, we may worry about losing what we have gained and the accompanying humiliation. Yet, if we recondition our mind to focus on what is really important, our perceptions, reactions and feelings will change.

Think of how much our reactions to winning and losing are based on cultural programming. Imagine that you are a person from one of three cultures: Italian, American Indian or American. If you are an Italian, it is acceptable to laugh and cry. If you are an American Indian, you may neither laugh nor cry. If you are an American, you may laugh but not cry.

Where, in this process of cultural conditioning, do we allow ourselves to *be the person we need to be*, both to achieve what we wish to achieve and to experience the happiness we desire. We need to break out of conditioned patterns and decide what is right for us. This includes the value we place on adversity, negative feedback and stress. Then, regardless of what happens, we still enjoy the challenge.

The Courage to Risk

I met Jim Lorentzen in 1970. Today Jim trains business people in Portland, Oregon, to use his concepts of "soft selling." Jim was once a workaholic. He admits his devotion to work became a problem:

> I became a one-dimensional person, neglecting the physical and spiritual sides of my life. Maybe my intensive work schedule is the reason why I developed Chronic Fatigue Syndrome. I've been sick for five years. My perseverance, which has been a major factor in my success, compounded my illness.
>
> My philosophy historically is that *achievers are successful because they form the habits that unsuccessful people avoid.* After thirty years of focusing on what I had to do to provide my desired life-style, I became ill. My illness has caused me to reexamine my values, and my life is now fuller. I told myself the only answer was to find the balance physically, financially, spiritually and in my relationships. Each day, after three or four hours of work, I hit the wall. I reassure myself of how fortunate I am that I have my own business. I'm also grateful that my illness is not as serious as is usually experienced with this affliction. Now I hike the Columbia Gorge.

We need to break out of our comfort zones.

It is important that we get out of our comfort zone. In childhood, we are taught to stay within the lines. Now we need to stretch ourselves. Early on we were conditioned to speak only when spoken to: "don't ask; wait for what you want to be offered to you." Succeeding in business requires that we resolve our fear of being rejected and begin to ask.

Going beyond our comfort zone and being risk-oriented requires that we control our fears. We need to do what we fear most. Often a negative thought, by itself, is not critical. It is the succession of negative thoughts that creates a chain reaction that gets us in trouble. We need to break the negative succession by instead repeating to ourselves "cancel, cancel."

We can allow our fears to immobilize us, or we can capitalize on what makes us feel insecure. Merely understanding our fears can neutralize their negative influence. The next step is to confront them in an effort to resolve them. Some of us may want to take the most aggressive approach and *attack our fears.*

Courageous Reactions

Audie Murphy was one of nine children growing up in the depression of the 1930s along the Oklahoma and Texas border. One day his father decided that feeding and clothing so many children was too much of an emotional strain, so he left. Audie's mother did the best she could, but the physical exhaustion ruined her health. By the time Audie turned sixteen, she had died.

Audie applied to the Marine Corps, but they would not consider such a "baby-faced kid." He tried the Air Force and was turned down for being underage. Then he lied to the Army and was accepted.

Audie excelled under pressure. In each battle his courage strengthened his reputation as the greatest hero of World War II. Possibly Audie's most heroic deed occurred late in the war. Audie and his men were told to take the top of a hill. Knee-deep in snow, they were in danger of dying from the cold or being killed by the enemy. They reached the top of the hill, only to find themselves being attacked by 200 soldiers and five tanks. Audie radioed for help, and two tanks were sent to protect them. One went into a ditch and could no longer function. The other was hit, began burning and was in danger of exploding. Audie, the senior man on the team, sent his men back and held the hill until they were safe.

Starting back, he passed through the smoke of the burning tank, and a thought intrigued him. He could see, in the flames, the machine gun on top of the tank. Wondering if the weapon was still operational, he climbed on top of the tank. It was working. For a moment the smoke cleared. In front of him was the enemy who had moved out into an open field. He then "wiped them out." The enemy tanks, without any soldiers for support, retreated. Audie had taken the hill against 200 enemy troops. Years later he explained his heroism: "I didn't have the guts to be a coward."

We all have fears. The challenge is how we react to what frightens us. Some of our greatest heroes may have been as frightened as any of us would be, but under pressure, they *reacted courageously.*

> **Successful people do what they fear most.**

18
Understand Rejection

> When we see our fears for what they are,
> they lose their negative power.

Only one word determines the difference between rejection that is amusing and rejection that is dangerous to our ego. The word is *personal*. The better we understand why we take rejection personally, the more easily we can capitalize on negative feedback. There are two kinds of rejection. One is an amusing experience, which we feel comfortable relaying to our friends. The incident seems funny to us. The second can cause ego damage, a loss of self-esteem and depression.

For example, you stop for a red light and notice that in the car alongside you, for no apparent reason, the person is sticking his tongue out at you. Does that upset you? Of course not. You think to yourself, "This person must have some sort of problem." However, under what circumstances might such an experience upset us? What if you knew the person? What if it was your spouse? What if it was your manager? What if it was your spouse and manager together?

Releasing Our Fears

If we understand our fears, we can more easily release them. As an analogy, we arrive home alone at midnight, concerned with our security. Our first reaction is to turn on the lights. While our fears are valid, we soon realize that we are safe.

Our fears are only voices. Some of these voices are positive. They warn us of possible danger. Others frighten us. Think of those fears that inhibit us from trying. When we fail, they say, "I told you so," and cause us to feel even more discouraged.

If we receive a telephone call and the voice tells us, "Why are you trying to succeed; you know you have no chance," we should hang up. Surely we would refuse to listen. If we were to listen, then hopefully we would not believe what the voice was saying. If we listen and believe what is being said, at least let's not do what the voice is telling us.

The more we "turn the lights on" our fears, the more easily we can separate those that prepare us for the challenge from those that prevent us from trying. As we recognize the malignant fears that try to consume us, we may see them for what they really are—only faceless voices which have no power except the influence we allow them to have upon us.

Self-Acceptance through Self-Sufficiency

When Patricia was ten years old, she was rated the most unpopular child in her fifth-grade class. She felt the reason for this thorough rejection was because she was different by being independent and not seeking peer group acceptance. Wondering why her teacher would have the class rate anyone on something so negative helped her detach from her hurt feelings and not take it so personally. Being rejected for being an outsider also reinforced self-reliance. Now she recognizes that her emotional independence limits personal relationships, and this upsets her.

Today Patricia Sperduto is a successful stockbroker for Morgan Stanley in New York City. The way she thinks about rejection assures her success:

> There is nothing life-threatening about rejection. It is only a game. I take winning seriously. Succeeding is a challenge, but losing does not matter. *The risk is not in failing but in being mediocre.*

When Trish was eighteen, her nineteen-year-old sister was killed by a car. This was the worst experience of her life. She explained the situation to me:

> I was totally devastated and overcome by horrible feelings. Her life had been lost, and I became determined not to waste mine. Our life is a gift that must be fulfilled. I competed for and won a scholarship. I was proving to myself that I could achieve whatever I decided I

wanted. You accept what you can't change and focus all your energy into what you can accomplish.

When my sister and I were children and went to our mother with problems, she would tell us, "Don't show me your problems. Show me how you are going to handle them." I became convinced that you cannot blame the world for your problems or let people upset you. Whenever anyone says "no" to me it's almost as if there is a chemical change in my body, creating energy that strengthens my will to win.

As a child Trish enjoyed reading biographies of successful athletes who had suffered defeat until they had nothing to lose. She described what she learned from these accounts:

When people realize that they can't go any lower is often when they make their move. Some things you can't change such as gravity. But when you have a chance, then, even though you feel emotionally exhausted, you take every shred of energy and focus on what you can change.

With this attitude she has exceeded her expectations and is now challenging herself to go beyond her present performance. The secret of her success is in her belief that "we can succeed in a financial world of constant chaos. Just take responsibility for what you can control. This attitude has allowed me to be more emotionally open. Interdependence creates and produces more than just being independent."

Tragedy Tempers Our Soul

Wilma, the seventeenth of nineteen children, was born in poverty to a store clerk and maid in Clarksville, Tennessee. As an infant she had scarlet fever and pneumonia. Then, when she was four, polio crippled her in one leg. Her parents drove one hundred miles to the nearest hospital where the doctors told them there was little that could be done.

Her family took turns massaging her leg for four hours each day. By six she could almost walk. She would hop, fall, laugh and try again. When she was eight, she received a leg brace. Her progress was slow but steady.

In 1960, at the age of twenty, she qualified for the Olympics in Rome in track. She won the 100 meters. She won her second gold medal in the 200 meters. No American woman had ever won three gold medals in the Olympics, but Wilma had the chance. She was running the anchor leg in the 400-meter relay.

Her team's passing of the baton was not what it should have been, and Wilma watched the German runner take the lead. However, Wilma was the fastest woman in the world, and her speed carried her to victory. Wilma Rudolph, referred to as a gazelle because of the way she ran, had won her third gold medal.

> **The risk is not in failing but in being mediocre.**

19

Becoming Emotionally Involved

> The stronger our self-image, the more easily
> we will capitalize on rejection.

There are three reasons why we take rejection personally. The first is emotional involvement. The second and third reasons are dealt with in the next two chapters. The question we need to ask ourselves is: *How emotionally involved can we become with someone before we assume the person knows us so well that whatever he or she says might be true, causing us to feel vulnerable to any possible rejection and therefore defensive?*

Imagine you become romantically involved, and your partner says to you, "I love you. I want to spend the rest of my life with you." This tends to enhance our self-image. We become involved with the person, experiencing love, intimacy and marriage, and the years pass. Then we wake up one morning, and our spouse says, "I now feel I know you very well, and I don't love you anymore."

How much time must pass before the ego heals from the trauma of such an experience? Six months? Maybe a few years? However, the desire to become involved again usually motivates us to find another relationship. Then, within our subconscious mind, a voice says, "Watch out. You might get hurt again." At that moment we might begin to subconsciously destroy the relationship. This is because we are often more relaxed with people whom we do not need; and the friendship is comfortable and permanent. Yet, the more important the other person becomes to us, the more vulnerable we are to rejection. For many people the solution is to end the relationship. The result is that we destroy what we might need most of all.

> **The better the relationship, the better the results.**

Our success, whether in love or money, is based on relationships. Relationships require emotional involvement. The more emotionally involved we become, the better the relationship. If, however, becoming emotionally involved causes us to feel vulnerable to rejection, we might become defensive. Being cautious with people prevents us from extending ourselves and minimizes our results. We are less likely to gain their agreement and have them accept our ideas.

Therefore, our success in business or in love depends on our ability to become emotionally involved. This requires disengaging our fear of rejection. We begin by recognizing why emotional involvement triggers our fear of being rejected.

Our Self-Image

There are two factors that determine at what point we take rejection personally. The first, as we have discussed, is emotional involvement, and the other is our self-image. As long as our self-image is greater than the emotional involvement, we will not take rejection personally. Instead we will think to ourselves, "If this person really knew me, she would love me," or "How can this person reject me when he does not even know me?"

Yet, the more emotionally involved we become, the more we feel the other person knows us better than we know ourselves. As the emotional involvement exceeds our self-image, all our assumptions may begin to change. We think to ourselves, "This person knows me so well that whatever he or she says about me might be true." Then we become defensive, fearful that any negative feedback will damage our self-image.

> **Our self-image determines our reactions to failure and rejection.**

Those who have a negative self-image and fail will think to themselves, "I never should have tried. I knew I would fail. All I've done is make a fool of myself."

If, instead, we have a strong self-image, we will think, "This is only a temporary setback. I deserve to succeed. Therefore, I need to find another way to get to where I want to be."

Even our reactions to success are reflections of our self-image. If we have a poor self-image, but somehow succeed, we will think to ourselves, "How did that happen? I must have been lucky. If I try again, I will probably fail and lose what I've gained. I better stay where I am and feel fortunate that I got as far as I did."

If we have a positive self-image and succeed, we will think, "I'm just getting warmed up. This success is only an example of how much better I can be."

The Positive Path

Recently I gave a lecture for IBM's customers in Montana and met Lisa Edelhoff with Physician Computer Network. She believes that her success in business is based on the following:

> I have had difficult relationships in my personal life and have had to overcome family strife. No matter what happens you stay together. Your commitment gives you the courage to deal with change and resolve the friction and anger. We all need to develop the courage to take the positive path.

Develop a reservoir of strength to eliminate the obstacles.

> The challenge is then in maintaining the strength. Today I am working off of that strength. I feel comfortable in confronting conflict by moving toward resolving disputes.

Therefore, the better our self-image, the less likely we will accept failure as a permanent way of life. Instead we will "do battle with it." We also will capitalize on success and move on to our next challenge, rather than feel lucky and become complacent.

Obviously, if we can improve our self-image, we will feel more confident when we become emotionally involved. We will believe that the only reason why people reject us is because they do not know us. We will decide that, if they are negative toward us, we have the responsibility to extend ourselves, so that they will know that we are worthy of their trust and respect. Gradually, our friendly confidence will disarm their resistance, and we will gain the desired relationships and results. The challenge is to develop such a strong self-image that rejection stimulates us to become more involved.

Staying in Balance

When my youngest son, David, turned eleven, he decided he was ready for an adult surfboard and wanted to earn the money by working for me. I told him to try selling my audiocassette program. He agreed and called on a stockbrokerage office in our neighborhood. He was dressed in his suit, wearing his Nikes, and carrying my briefcase.

Later he told me of his experience. He asked the secretary if he could see the manager. Rather than speaking to David she began laughing and just pointed in the direction of the manager's office. When he walked into the office, he introduced himself and gave the line that he had prepared, "I would like you to try this audiocassette program, which can help your brokers deal with rejection so that when they come home at night they are not depressed."

The manager asked him how old he was, and David told him. The manager then explained, "I have a son who is eleven years old," as though wondering why his son was not making business calls. Then he said, "Dave, I'll make a deal with you. Come back and speak to my brokers at our next meeting. Just tell them what you told me, and I promise I'll buy a set from you."

A few weeks later David spoke to the manager and his eight brokers. Five paid for the audio program, and David earned his surfboard. For David the presentation was the same as surfing. He was on the edge and in danger of wiping out, but he knew if he kept his balance he would enjoy himself.

Accepting Ourselves

Realize how easily our self-image can be influenced by other people's comments. For most of us achievement without recognition is depressing. We need the applause and acceptance of others to be able to accept ourselves. Acceptance becomes a primary need, and the opposite, rejection, becomes the demotivator. We need to feel good enough about ourselves that we can capitalize on negative feedback, rather than taking rejection personally.

How emotionally involved can you become with people before you begin taking their negative feedback personally? How might that affect your relationships, not just in business but in your personal life? We need to be aware of that moment in a relationship in which we become too concerned with the reactions of the other person. Then we need to decide what we will do to pursue our objective, even though feeling vulnerable to rejection.

> **Become emotionally involved.**

> **Develop strong relationships.**

> **Decide we deserve the success.**

20
Frequency of Rejection

During periods of disappointment, we can still pursue our goals.

While the first reason we take rejection personally is emotional involvement, the second is the frequency of negative feedback. How much failure and rejection can we persevere through before we start taking it personally? Of course, we can handle rejection. One of the reasons why we are as successful as we are is because we can deal with rejection. The question is, how much negative feedback can we experience before it starts to get to us?

The depth of our resiliency determines how long we can persevere.

Succeeding in business often requires becoming involved with people who are unreceptive to us. Our success depends on our ability to persevere through considerable rejection. As an example, when we are starting our own business we may need to contact people who are often resistant to us. Each of us, to some degree, can deal with rejection. Yet most everyone of us can only experience so much negative feedback before we start taking it personally.

Often we work with prospective clients who are hostile toward us. How many times will we follow up on a qualified prospect before we do not want to hear any more negative feedback?

Park City, Utah once made many men wealthy because of silver. I once took a tour of a silver mine, which had originally been owned by a bank clerk. He had been particularly precise in creating the mine, but, after exhausting himself financially and without success, he sold his deed. The new owner went only 25 feet further and found $27 million worth of this precious metal.

Sometimes success is so close, but we feel beaten by continuous disappointment. Often, with just a few more attempts we will succeed.

Fear of rejection also applies to engaging groups of people. Most of us feel inhibited speaking to many people at one time, while a conversation with one person might feel very comfortable. We know that the more people we speak to at one time, the greater the likelihood that one person might be negative. If we cannot resolve the objection, then we may feel embarrassed for having "wiped out" in front of so many people.

Our vulnerability to being rejected also occurs in social gatherings. For example, most of us will admit that attending a cocktail party can be an inhibiting experience, particularly if we arrive last and do not know anyone. Why are we fearful? Possibly we are concerned that, if we were to join a few people, one might say to us, "I'm sorry, but this is confidential."

We might decide to never go to a cocktail party again without first having a couple of drinks. Before we leave, however, we may notice one person alone. We can decide to make one last effort. We introduce ourselves, and the person says to us, "I'm sorry, this is confidential." This negative reaction would probably not upset us. We might even be amused by their comment, thinking to ourselves, "How can this person reject me, since no one is accepting him?"

However, we might be unaware that the group of people we had approached were discussing a personal matter that they didn't care to share with anyone else in the room. Meanwhile, the person who was alone may have simply been lost in thought and in the process of making some major life decisions. The point is, their unapproachability would have had nothing to do with us as people.

Often our reactions are not based on reality, on how people actually feel about us, but on our own self-image and ego resiliency. We each have to ask ourselves, "How much rejection can I experience at one time before my feelings are hurt?" Then we must decide how we are going to pursue our objective, even though feeling vulnerable.

> **Rejection can make us more resilient.**

Channeling Our Fears

He was five years old, an angelic-looking child, living in England. One day his father asked him to take a note to the police station. The police officer decided to follow the instructions written on the note. He took the child through a series of corridors to an open cell, locked him in and left him there. After about fifteen minutes, the officer returned and explained to him, "This is what happens to naughty boys." Then he let him go home.

Maybe there were factors other than just this incident that caused the boy to become neurotic. In any event, as time passed he realized he was becoming psychotic. Desperately he sought a way to keep his sanity. In time he discovered how to relieve himself of the emotional pressure caused by his fears. Alfred Hitchcock's ability to channel his fears into creative achievement also created his success.

We all have fears. Some of our fears can save us, such as convincing us that we should not walk in a dangerous neighborhood late at night. If we were fearless, we might be oblivious to possible danger.

Many of us, once we succeed, lose our fear of failing. We begin to believe we are destined for success without working for it. This can happen to a boxer who, thrilled with winning the championship, does not train hard enough for his next bout. As another example, some of us, if we succeed in business, often believe we have the King Midas touch, and whatever we touch will turn to gold. Then we wonder why our next business venture fails.

If we are driving down a hill and we have no brakes, we could be in serious trouble. The purpose of our brakes is not always to stop but to slow us down so that we arrive safely.

Similarly, the purpose of our fears might be to prevent us from hurting ourselves. Positive fears are designed to slow us down so we can see more clearly what is happening. Rather than causing us to stop, our fears can merely help us to arrive at our destination more safely and therefore assure our success.

Often we might disregard our fears and fail be cause we are unprepared for adversity. Our assumption that we will succeed can cause so many blind spots that we do not see the risks involved. Then, defeated and disappointed later on, we decide that trying was a mistake. As a result, for the remainder of our lives, we might seek only comfortable situations.

Our positive fears can keep our enthusiasm in balance. The problem occurs when our negative fears become too powerful and prevent us from developing our potential. When our fears take away our pleasure—as though life were a great banquet that we are not allowed to taste—we must consider the ways in which we can free ourselves from our own psychological imprisonment.

Managing Our Fears

We take control of our destiny by managing our fears. We separate those that can help us from those that are self-defeating. Too often we allow our fears to convince us that we should avoid challenging situations. Instead, we need to talk ourselves into making the effort.

There is the true story of a high school football team that was losing 28 to 0 at halftime. When they returned to the field for the second half, they became heroic. With five touchdowns they won the game 35 to 28. After the victory celebration the coach was asked what he had said at halftime that had so influenced his players. He explained, "I told them, `If you lose, I will still love you. If you lose, your mothers will still love you. But I'm not sure about your girlfriends.'"

Just as we can be inspired by the motivational talk of others, we can be motivated by our own self-talk. We can make our lives into whatever we wish, validating our perceptions and fulfilling our dreams.

Consider two factors for success. The first is the enthusiasm we bring to the challenge. Being psychologically motivated to achieve an objective is crucial. The second factor is far more important—*our ability to react under pressure.* Many of us become enthusiastic when taking on a new adventure. Unfortunately, our enthusiasm can be dangerous if it pushes us into situations that we cannot deal with emotionally or psychologically. We may then find ourselves on the downside of an emotional roller coaster. The courage to react under pressure becomes a primary factor in our success.

As an illustration, there was a professor who lectured to scientists on a complex subject. His chauffeur would wait for him in the back of the room. On one occasion, as they were driving away, the chauffeur commented, "Professor, I believe I have heard your presentation so frequently that I now remember every word. If ever you are not feeling well, I think I can give the lecture for you."

The professor took the suggestion negatively, and an argument ensued. Finally he said to his chauffeur, "If you believe you're so good, you're on tomorrow morning."

The chauffeur immediately agreed. The next morning the professor sat in the back of the room, wearing the chauffeur's uniform. The chauffeur, dressed in the professor's suit, gave the presentation with accuracy, enthusiasm and confidence.

As the applause subsided, the master of ceremonies stepped to the lectern and said, "Great speech. In fact, we still have time for questions. Are there any?"

The first question was complex and profound, but the chauffeur reacted quickly, "I cannot believe, in an audience of this sophistication, that a question so simple could be asked. In fact, to show you how simple it is, my chauffeur in the back of the room will answer it."

He was willing to take on a new challenge, as we need to be, but more important, he had the ability to react under pressure.

Our resiliency determines our tolerance for rejection.

Difficult experiences allow us to discover our resourcefulness.

Positive fears prepare us for the obstacles in our path.

More important than the temporary excitement of enthusiasm is our permanent ability to react under pressure.

21

Improving
Our
Self-Image

If we improve our self-image, we can confidently
confront greater challenges.

The third and last reason why we take rejection personally comes from
our feelings of inadequacy. For many of us there are people who make us
feel inadequate. Possibly their age, position or title cause us to believe
that whatever they say might be true, including their opinion of us.

More specifically, most of us are completely ourselves with people we
feel comfortable around. With such persons we are both aggressive and
friendly. If we consider that someone is more important than we are, we
might lose our balance. We may continue to be warm and friendly but
give up our aggressive and confident attitude. Somehow we have decided that whatever this person might say about us could be valid,
which causes us to feel vulnerable to rejection.

Looking at this another way, we can say we have three personalities.
Our first personality comes out in the way we are with people we feel
are not as successful as us. We may not want to admit to such social
snobbery, yet if invited to a party, we might find an excuse not to go,
claiming, "They're not my kind of people. I might get bored."

As an illustration, if we were walking along the street and disregarded someone who asked us for a quarter, and we were cursed as we

walked away, would that bother us? Probably not, because in our mind this person is not a judge of what we are worth. Therefore, our first personality is the "who" we are with people we feel are in a lesser position.

Our second personality is who we are with people we feel are our peers. With such individuals we are both aggressive and friendly. If one of them were critical of us, we might think to ourselves, "I am as good as this person. The criticism is really positive feedback that can help me make changes in my course of direction. This is an opportunity to improve myself!" Therefore, the negative feedback from this kind of person can help us become more effective in dealing with similar situations in the future.

Then there is the third part of our personality—who we are when we react to people we feel are more successful than we are. With them we may become cautious and defensive.

As another illustration of our three personalities, think of the old television program *The Honeymooners,* with Jackie Gleason. The character Ralph had three personalities. With his wife Alice and his friend Ed Norton, he could be insensitive and abusive. With his friends at work he was gregarious and charming. With his boss he was shy and apprehensive. We need to recognize that these same three patterns may apply to ourselves.

Positive Patterns

Understanding the relationship between our self-image and our reactions to others helps us recognize why we are comfortable with some people and uncomfortable with others. Our challenge is to disengage from our unconscious, sometimes self-defeating, reaction. Then we can develop patterns that improve our self-image.

In 1972, an IBM sales representative contacted me. He had just been assigned a territory of 50 qualified prospects, with no existing customers. He felt comfortable contacting 48 of the prospects, but he did not understand why he was avoiding two prospective customers.

During the conversation, he told me that the 48 he was contacting were small companies and the decision makers were purchasing agents and accountants. The two he was avoiding were large and, according to the previous sales representative, the contact within both companies was the president.

I asked him how he felt when calling on purchasing agents of small companies, and he said, "No problem. I feel I am as good as they are." Then I asked him why he was avoiding these two major prospects. After a long pause, he said, "I feel that anyone who is the president of a company of that size must be a very important person. Just the thought of calling on someone at that level makes me apprehensive." Yet, with that honesty, he made the calls to these key contacts and went well over his quota.

If we fail, but no one knows about it, then the failure is not that serious. For many of us, *it is not the failure that upsets us, but the rejection.* "Looking bad in the eyes of others" becomes the problem.

Frequency of Adversity

When adversity occurs more frequently than we expected then we may begin to assume that we are the cause of our misfortune. The solution is to realize that the frequency of failure is part of the process of succeeding.

> The chances of success increase with the frequency of our efforts.

Theodor S. Geisel wrote a book for children entitled *And to Think that I Saw it on Mulberry Street.* He described what happened after he was rejected by the 23rd publisher:

> I found myself lugging the manuscript up Madison Avenue, heading for my apartment, where I was going to dump the thing in the incinerator.... I bumped into a long-unseen college friend, Mike McClintock.
> Mike said, "What are you doing these days?"
> I said, "I'm an unsuccessful author of children's books. What are you doing these days?"
> And Mike said, "I am an editor of children's books. We're standing right in front of my office. Why don't we step inside."
> Twenty minutes later I became a legitimate author with a contract.

Today children and adults enjoy the stories of Theodor S. Geisel, better known as Dr. Seuss.

> We create our fate by positioning ourselves.

Six Alexander Fleming was a British bacteriologist working in St. Mary's Hospital in London in 1928. One day he forgot to cover some petri dishes that contained bacteria. An airborne mold landed in one dish and began to grow, inhibiting the growth of the bacteria. Sir Fleming had discovered penicillin. We might decide that his discovery was based on luck rather than his own effort. Yet, if we keep opening windows, we increase our opportunities. The more consistent our efforts, the more we improve our opportunities for success.

Emotional Involvement

When we feel that someone has a greater awareness of who we are than we have of ourselves, we will assume that their opinion of us is valid. This makes us vulnerable to any negative comments, until our only desire is to protect our ego rather than extend ourselves.

The Other Person

If we respect the other person more than ourselves, then we will tend to believe what he or she says. Any negative comment this person voices we will take personally.

There are three ways we may react, depending on our image of ourselves and of others. First, if we feel superior we might be unconcerned when people don't accept us. We may even react aggressively. Second, with those people who we feel are our equal, we will usually take their feedback to heart. Though any rejection might be upsetting, we will probably combine our desire for friendship with our competitive spirit and react pleasantly. Third, when we feel dependent or subservient, our reactions to any negative feedback will usually be defensive. Our assumption that such people know what they are talking about causes us to become oversensitive and react cautiously.

"Over Our Heads" and Avoiding Opportunity

Some of us "get ourselves in over our heads" by taking on challenges in areas in which we are not yet proficient. If we "worked our way up the ladder," our proficiency might eventually match the challenge. We need to evaluate our present skills and appraise the complexity of the responsibilities we confront.

A more serious error is to avoid significant opportunities because our self-image is not equal to the challenge. Rather than "selling ourselves short," we need the courage to change.

Courage

An acorn becomes an oak tree naturally, just as a kitten becomes a cat, but we do not become the person we were destined to be automatically. For us the process of developing our potential requires a very different ingredient—*courage*. This quality has two parts. The first is having *the courage to be honest* with ourselves. It is not easy to admit our own frailties, such as the reasons why we take failure and rejection personally.

The second part is having *the courage to suffer*. In other words, we must be willing to experience failure, rejection and anxiety so that we can bridge the gap from where we are to where we need to be. If we can capitalize on stress, we can develop our potential, enhance our self-image and increase our self-esteem.

In 1991 Albert Brooks made a movie entitled *Defending Your Life*. In the movie the hero dies in an automobile accident and goes to Judgment City, where he is to be judged as to whether he will go back to earth or move on. The determining factor is his courage. If he allows his fears to prevent him from developing his potential, he has to go back to earth. As the character, played by Albert Brooks, reaches out and capitalizes on existing opportunities, regardless of his fears, he is able to move on.

Our fears cause our vulnerabilities, which create our limitations. By attacking our fears, our vulnerabilities can stimulate us to break through our psychological barriers. This is because our fears generate energy. If we attack the fear, the energy can then be used as an added force to keep us active and productive.

> **We courageously attack our fears and move on to the next level.**

Sometimes we need the courage to recover from the heartache of a great loss. Theodore Roosevelt, as a young man, suffered through the death of his wife. In this tragic period he felt he would never again find purpose in his life. Emotionally overwhelmed, he wrote these poignant words: "Fair, pure and joyous as a maiden, loving, tender and happy as a young wife. When she had just become a mother, when her life seemed to be just begun, and when the years seemed so bright before her, then, by a strange and terrible fate, death came to her. And when my heart's dearest died, the light went from life forever." Theodore Roosevelt was both a man of compassion and resiliency. Though heartbroken, he was able to move on and achieve great things. Each of us needs to identify how we will recover from tragic events, as well as from the daily challenges stemming from difficult times and difficult people.

> If we improve our self-image, we can comfortably deal with people in more important positions.

> The courage to admit our vulnerabilities helps us to change.

> The courage to experience stress can assure our continuous growth.

> As we open windows of opportunity, we increase the chances of our success.

22
Capitalize on Negative Feedback

Have the courage to persevere through rejection with dignity.

We can learn a lesson from the way in which migrating birds avoid becoming wet from the rain during a storm. Rather than hide or seek shelter, these birds fly above the clouds. Much the same way, when moving through a storm toward our target, we can raise our self-image and ascend above the hostility of others. When we decide, "I am precious and of value," the rejection, regardless of its validity, is always helpful.

Seeing the Positive in Rejection

If the rejection is valid, then we want to know what we have done to cause this person's reactions. Negative feedback is valuable in guiding us toward our target. The objectivity of others can help us make changes in our course. Their critical feedback instructs us to modify

our direction and might even direct us into avenues of greater opportunity.

When I first began lecturing professionally in 1967, I would always
ask people, after the session had ended, "How can I do better?" They
would often comment that I was too serious and that I needed to bring
some humor into my presentation. Yet I was reluctant to even try being
humorous.

I realized that my fear of rejection was inhibiting me. I knew that if I
did not tell the joke well, I would be embarrassed. There I was, giving
lectures on how to overcome the fear of rejection, and I was allowing my
own insecurities to hinder my lecturing ability. I decided to confront my
fears. I would think of jokes I had enjoyed and practice on my friends. I
would read humorous quotes in newspapers and tell them to neighbors.
I would think of embarrassing situations I had experienced and discuss
them with relatives.

When people were amused by certain jokes, quotes and personal
episodes, I would introduce them into my next presentation. Gradually,
my serious lectures were enhanced by these entertaining illustrations.

The humor has so improved my talks that I have been recently asked
to speak in Australia, the Bahamas, Bermuda, Canada, England,
Mexico, Singapore and Spain. I never would have achieved this success
if I had not asked for criticism. If we are making errors, we want to hear
about them. Negative feedback provides information that enables us to
modify our strategy and become more effective.

Then there is invalid or unwarranted rejection, in which people are
taking their frustrations out on us. If we determine that their hostility
has nothing to do with us, then we will not take it personally.

If ever again a person is negative toward us, we need to ask them,
"Could you tell me what I said to upset you so that I will not make the
same error in the future, or are you having a bad day, and just taking
your frustrations out on me?" Whether valid or invalid, we want to understand the cause of their hostility. Only then can we capitalize on their
negative feelings.

Disengaging Our Ego

Another solution for dealing with rejection also relates to birds, as in
"water off a duck's back." In other words, if we cannot fly above the rejection, then we need to "disengage our ego."

I met Dave Raia in 1978 when he was a training manager for Illinois
Bell. One of his projects included recording my presentation onto video-

tape for his company. Today Dave is the general operations manager for the AT&T Denver national service center. His 25-year AT&T gold watch is now a year old.

Many years ago, Dave made a correct decision, but the way he implemented his idea irritated a few people including his boss, so he was fired. He described his situation:

> I was emotionally destroyed. I was good at my work. I enjoyed the job. More than needing the money, I also needed the sense of purpose. I just couldn't deal with defeat. I refused to accept the failure. I found myself unable to leave. I would come to work each morning, and they wanted to know what I was doing. I told them that I had to do my job because there was work I had not yet completed. They might have fired me and were not paying me, but I wasn't finished. They didn't know what to do with me.

> | We must refuse to accept failure. |

> They decided, since I wouldn't leave and I was working without pay, that firing me was cruel and unusual punishment. They rescinded the termination and instead gave me a week without pay. More important than the relief I felt in getting back my job was the strategies I developed. I learned that my response to provocative stimuli could cause me to use poor judgment. The solution was to keep my management decisions on a win-win basis. I also believe in Peter Drucker's philosophy that he would never promote people into a top level job who had not made some mistakes. Otherwise they are sure to be mediocre.

> The most profound experience in my youth occurred in my senior year of high school. I was taking so many classes and participating in so many sports that I was reducing my total effectiveness. I decided to drop one activity and quit the basketball team. Some of my friends criticized me, as though my decision had made me a quitter. I decided then that it was important never to give up. Ever since then I have refused to quit.

> | Seek tranquility in the midst of tragedy. |

> My refusal to ever accept failure has had unfortunate repercussions. My wife and I have six children. We lost our first child. I was so emotionally upset that I beat my fists on a tree. I tore the bark off while tearing the skin off my hands. I then made an act of will never to "feel" again. For good or ill I have few emotional attachments. While

this prevents me from being emotionally uplifted, some people do accuse me of having a frightening grasp on reality. There are benefits to being emotionally detached such as tranquility, sobriety and serenity.

The preferable solution is to *improve our self-image,* so that we are able to use rejection, whether valid or invalid, for our benefit. In this way we can be both emotionally involved and ego-involved. However, we need to understand that our self-image lives in our ego. If we begin taking rejection personally, then our self-image is in danger of becoming damaged. In order to protect our self-image, we need to detach our ego, though continuing to stay involved emotionally.

Psychological Solutions

There are two ways to survive rejection: First, we can improve our self-image. If the rejection is valid, we need to make changes. If the rejection is invalid, we need to realize that the other person's hostility is not our problem. Second, we can disengage our ego.

Can we be emotionally involved with someone while, in the same moment, being ego-detached? Not easily, but it can be done. As an analogy, there are three types of moviegoers. When violence and trauma occur, the first person says, "It's only a movie! That's called special effects. That actor is being paid to go through that." The second person is temporarily traumatized. The best situated is the third person, who has the ability to become emotionally involved with the movie and feel what is happening, but not be traumatized by it. The objective is to *become fascinated with human behavior,* particularly the origins of hostility. Then, if ever again people are angry with us, we can become more involved to determine why they are irritated.

As a second analogy, imagine being a star in a Broadway show. On a given morning, we are informed that someone we love dearly has passed away. The hours drift by, and our depression deepens. It is now eight o'clock in the evening and curtain call. The lights in the theater dim, the curtains rise, and the music starts. Do we have the ability to "flip a switch" in our head and, suddenly, "be on"? This is a primary quality in successful people that is missing in most others.

> We must develop the ability to be, not the person we are,
> but the person we need to be.

As a final analogy, we can neither see the wind nor touch it. Yet we can feel it and its power. It can uproot trees and carry away houses and cars. We want to become the wind. We want to feel what people feel without their being able to damage us. We want to move people but not have them hurt us.

Which analogy do we prefer? We can become the wind, be on stage, flipping a switch in our head, or be an emotionally involved moviegoer without being traumatized by what we see. We feel what people feel, but they cannot touch us.

People who are successful in business have usually suffered through difficult times in their personal life. Ann Miller was with Digital Equipment for five years, then Price Waterhouse, and five years with Arthur Young. She told me how she has coped with adversity:

> I married early, had a child and divorced a few years later. After a few personal challenges, along with business failure, nothing ever seems to be that big of a deal.
>
> Often our success is based on habit. You do whatever has to be done and, once you succeed, the process becomes a habit. The failures become easier. After my divorce I was fired and found myself stranded in a foreign country. Yet I have this ingrained belief that as long as I have my health, my intelligence and my desire to achieve, I have all I need.

Today, Ann is a regional manager for Applied Business Technology and is responsible for overseeing the sales and marketing effort of six offices in fifteen states. She has remarried, and her children are now three, four and twenty-three.

> Stressful situations get in the way. You can't get caught up with the secondary responsibilities that can cause you to overdose. You need to disengage from the irrelevant and carry on with the business at hand. You can develop a very positive perspective when you feel you are floating above it all. Certainly, when dealing with fear of failure, we need a strong self-image and the ability to control our reactions to adversity. These become lessons well learned in our quest for success.

> We must keep our self-esteem in the middle of the storm.

In 1910 Branch Rickey was a coach of a college baseball team. One night, when he and his players arrived in a small town in Indiana for a game, the hotel denied the only black player a room. Branch, in an effort to solve the problem and knowing that every other hotel in the town had the same policy, asked for a cot to be placed in his room for this one man. Although the hotel manager was displeased, he agreed.

Branch Rickey never forgot that young man, sitting on the cot, crying until his whole body shook. Somehow, Branch decided that night he would do what he could to eliminate such injustice.

Thirty-three years later, when he became an executive for the Brooklyn Dodgers, he persuaded the directors to have a black man on the team. The challenge was to find a man who was more than a good baseball player or even a potentially great player. He needed to find a man who was unique in that he would have two crucial qualities that were opposite.

First, this man would have to put up with verbal abuse and hostility, not just from the fans and sportswriters, but possibly from his own teammates. He would have to be silent in a terrible storm. If he retaliated, the problem would only worsen. Second, he had to be a man of dignity and self-respect with a competitive spirit.

People who have dignity do not accept abuse. Those who put up with abuse usually lack self-respect. Somehow this man would have to accept the hostility while keeping his dignity and self-respect.

Branch Rickey decided that man was Jackie Robinson. In their first meeting in 1946 he spoke to Jackie about the single factor that would determine the success or failure of what was then referred to as a "noble experiment." Branch said to him, "Jackie, the runs you score will not count. Only one quality will count. I have to ask you, do you have the courage?"

Jackie was denied the right to enter hotels and restaurants and verbally abused by the fans and even some of his own teammates. He suffered, yet persevered. Rather than allow the unkindness of others to take away his chance for greatness, he stayed resilient. He did not allow them to change his image of himself. Rather he changed their image of him.

In the Spring of 1947, a black man was not allowed to play in major league baseball but only in what was then referred to as the "Negro leagues."

In October of that year Jackie Robinson played in the World Series against the New York Yankees, and when the season ended, he was voted Rookie of the Year. After Jackie came Satchel Paige, Hank Aaron, Bob Gibson, Reggie Jackson, and Ricky Henderson—all because with self-respect Robinson had persevered through the rejection.

Jackie Robinson is a hero for everyone for his suffering and what he accomplished. If he could keep his dignity while thousands were rejecting him, then surely we can stay resilient in a storm. If one man can change the attitude of an entire nation, then we can change our attitude toward rejection.

> When we improve our self-image, then rejection is always helpful.

> Negative feedback guides us toward our target.

23
Charisma

> Our performance elicits the reaction from people
> that creates the experience we desire.

Managing Ourselves

There are three aspects of our lives that we need to manage: our *thoughts, feelings* and *behavior*. First, we need to manage the way we think. If our thoughts are positive, we are more likely to be confident and enthusiastic.

Yet positive thinking can be dangerous. If we do not recognize the potential for defeat, then we may be emotionally shocked by any adversity we confront. It is important to understand how our optimism can blind us to potential trouble. We need to acknowledge the benefits of thinking objectively.

Procrastination and Panic

Think of how often we procrastinate. In our college days, when a term paper was due in ten weeks, we often started working on the assignment the night before. Then by sunrise, stimulated by caffeine and candy bars, we were often brilliant! Therefore, negative thinking can be healthy if it creates a sense of urgency that forces us to become productive. *Panic breaks procrastination.*

Positive or negative thinking is not our concern. What is important is *our ability to manage our thinking.* Sometimes negative thinking can stimulate us. If we are avoiding a challenge because we do not want to confront an uncomfortable situation, then thinking of how our lives might become more difficult might force us into action. Thinking negatively may create anxiety. The secret for us is *managing anxiety* effectively. More specifically, *we convert anxiety into a creative force for achievement,* which initiates a positive momentum. By channeling energy from stress into productive activities we become more successful.

The Behavioral Solution

Yet, even when we have difficulty managing our thoughts and feelings, we can still succeed. We have one last chance. We need to *manage the way we behave.*

Shirley MacLaine explains, "If I knew I was going to go through something unpleasant, I invented an attitude that enabled me to handle it positively. Slowly I began to understand that when I was depressed or angry at a particular circumstance, it was because I had chosen to adopt that attitude. In other words, I made the choice. I believe that we each enact our own personal dramas in life according to what we want to experience."

We learn from Shirley MacLaine that life and the stage are synonymous. They are both dramas. When we decide that our life is a drama, nothing can trouble us. When we are on stage and playing a role, adversarial situations become merely soap operas that replace the danger of boredom with amusement. If our attitude causes us to become depressed or angry by the events of our lives, then our reactions will, in various ways, upset people. Their responses will usually be negative and only increase our frustrations.

Instead, we need to follow this three-step process:

1. *Perform* so that we
2. *Elicit the reaction* from people which
3. *Creates the experience* we desire.

> The best way to predict the future is to create it.

We predict the future as we wish it to be. Then we create the experiences that fulfill the prediction. The best way to create the experience is to elicit the reaction. Our *performance* gains *the desired response* from people, which *fulfills the prophecy.* Therefore, even if we have a negative attitude or feel depressed, we can still *perform* in a way that *gains* the *response* that *creates the desired experience.*

Understanding Our Reactions

There are two negative ways to behave when rejected. If we understand which of these two we are most likely to use when people are hostile toward us, then we may recognize ways to change our behavior. The first negative reaction to rejection is to stop trying. In this pattern we are oversensitive, cautious and retreating.

The second negative reaction is less frequent but more provocative—to counterattack and "straighten people out." If we are not sure of which reaction we are most likely to use, then we can try the following test. Assuming that you are familiar with the *Peanuts* cartoon, which person would you prefer to be if your only choices were Charlie Brown or Lucy?

If you prefer to be Charlie, then you are probably the warm, sensitive type who easily develops a rapport with people. We can tell Charlie whatever we wish, and he will never use it against us. However, Charlie is so afraid of rejection from the little red-haired girl that he cannot even talk to her. Meanwhile, Lucy has no problem taking the initiative. She will persevere forever, but she is often insensitive and upsets others.

We all know people who are similar to Charlie. Such people are loving and kind but are often oversensitive and take rejection too much to heart. They avoid confrontation, can be taken advantage of, and become depressed when people are cruel. Then there are people like Lucy, who, merely on the suspicion that someone might attack them, will attack first.

How do we react to rejection? Do we become oversensitive and defensive like Charlie Brown or counterattack and become hostile like Lucy?

Of course, there are those of us who are like Snoopy. We fly above the clouds, fighting the Red Baron, and disregarding all the trivia that might otherwise upset us. While we might be happy, we may be oblivious to certain parts of our reality. Though immune to rejection, we may not recognize when people feel negatively toward us.

Now, what changes might we make in the way we deal with rejection to become more successful? The antidote to rejection is *charisma.*

> Charisma is the balancing of opposite qualities within ourselves so that most anyone can relate to us.

What qualities might each of us need to develop to create that balance? We can begin to create charisma for ourselves by answering two questions. First, what do you feel is Lucy's primary strength? Then, what do you believe to be Charlie Brown's primary quality? Now, we take these two qualities and rephrase them. For example, *attack nicely* or *react pleasantly.* As an exercise in developing charismatic balance, select one quality from each of the following two columns:

Aggressively	Friendly
Confidently	Sensitive
Persistently	Humble
Tenaciously	Warm
Decisively	Compassionate
Relentlessly	Pleasant
Assertively	Kind

In other words, we want to be *aggressively sensitive, relentlessly compassionate* and *tenaciously warm.* Balance is the answer.

In the martial arts of jujitsu, if we are attacked by someone, we do not counterattack, stand there and take it or run away. Rather, we just step aside. The hostility is never confronted but just passes on by. When we are attacked verbally, we can follow a similar process:

1. *We react with concern* by asking questions such as, "What has happened to you that you are so upset with me?" As we allow people to express their negative feelings, their hostility will gradually

2. *Dissipate,* until they become

3. *Disarmed* and, therefore,

4. *Receptive* to our suggestions.

Eliminating resistance and gaining receptivity sets the stage for developing an ideal relationship, which enhances our chances of gaining our desired results.

Steve Drozdeck told me how he handled one situation:

> On one occasion, I was prospecting from one office to the next. I watched while the secretary took my card to the executive and, from behind the frosted glass windows, I could see him tear up my card. When she returned, I asked her to tell him that I had seen what happened. She came back and handed me a nickel, saying he was paying for the card. I gave her another card and told her to explain to him, "They're two for a nickel."

Steve has the ability to respond so pleasantly that he disarms people. He can think creatively and react quickly because he expects frequent rejection. Each of us, as we watch successful people, need to develop our own approach to ensuring our success.

We must develop the ability to manage our thoughts, feelings and behavior.

Charisma is the balancing of aggressiveness and sensitivity so that most anyone can both relate to and respect us.

24
Relationships and Results

> The sensitivity of the issue determines the required depth of the rapport.

There are two objectives we need to achieve to succeed in business. One is developing good relationships, and the other is getting results. Strengthening relationships increases results. Our ability to develop strong relationships requires fulfilling three responsibilities.

Developing the Relationship

Our first two responsibilities are (1) establishing rapport and (2) determining needs. The more complex a person's needs, the more we need to first develop rapport. We have to earn the right to ask questions if we want people to express their real concerns and feelings.

Imagine that we are in an elevator with a stranger. We would probably feel comfortable asking the person what the weather is like outside. However, we might create a problem if we were to ask, "Sir, you don't look so good. You seem to have been drinking. Are there any personal problems you would like to discuss with me?"

The more sensitive the subject we wish to discuss, the greater the rapport must be. Asking a stranger a question regarding the weather is not a very intimate encounter, but asking people about their personal problems usually requires a significant degree of rapport.

As an illustration, the youngest of my four children is now twenty-four. In spite of their ages, I usually challenge at least one of them in some way each day. Frequently, my child reacts by saying, "No, Dad, I don't want to discuss this with you."

In that moment I realize that the issue I am attempting to discuss is far more sensitive for my child than I realized or the rapport is not as good as I thought. I have two solutions:

- *Reduce the sensitivity of the issue.* In other words, I might say, "Okay. I'll drop the subject, but could we at least discuss this one small part?"

- *Increase the rapport.* For example, "Okay, but how about dinner this weekend, just you and me, so that I can at least tell you why I am so concerned."

Creating Receptivity

When people say to us, "What right do you have to ask me that kind of question?" they are actually saying, "You have not earned the right to ask me." However, when people feel that we sincerely care about them, they will usually relax and become responsive to us.

People love to talk about themselves if they feel comfortable with us. This becomes our challenge, to create the kind of rapport that causes people to want to express their inner feelings. In this way we gain insight into their needs and frustrations. The sensitivity of the issue we wish to discuss determines how much rapport we first need to establish.

The quality we must bear in mind in determining someone's needs is *understanding.* Consider, for example, our personal life, such as a love relationship. Of what value is love without understanding? When we are in conflict with someone we love and we understand why the person is behaving as he or she is, the understanding can replace our frustration with sympathy.

Once, in presenting my lecture, a man interrupted with a question that seemed inappropriate. During the break, I asked the manager why this person was so different. He informed me that his son was having brain surgery the next day for a tumor, and he had no idea what the outcome might be. Any negative feelings that I may have had toward him were instantly gone. We never should assume why a person is negative, but instead take the time to understand his or her motive.

Once we understand the person's needs we can then develop and *present solutions*. The primary quality required to fulfill this third responsibility is the ability to help people.

In review, the three responsibilities we have in gaining an ideal relationship are *establishing the rapport* necessary *to understand people's needs*, so that we can *help* them with possible *solutions*.

Getting Results

Our second primary objective is getting results. In raising children, we want them to get good grades. In business, we want to do well financially. Getting the desired results requires fulfilling another three responsibilities.

1. The first objective in getting results is to *describe reality*.

Imagine we have established a rapport and determined the person's needs. What we believe people need might be very different from what they think they need. There is no point in presenting solutions until we gain agreement regarding what their needs might be.

In politics, for example, the challenger cannot replace the incumbent if people are comfortable with the present administration. Even if problems exist and the majority of the public is frustrated, change still might not occur for fear that any change would only compound the problem. Therefore, the challenger will succeed only if he or she can convince the public of the severity of the situation and assure the voters that only through change will they be more comfortable. This is a difficult task. The incumbent has an advantage because people feel secure with the status quo.

Once people decide to change, either because we have gained their agreement regarding their needs or disturbed them regarding the severity of their problems, we are then ready to present solutions. However, when presenting solutions, we must be prepared to resolve objections. Thus the following:

2. The second responsibility in gaining results is to overcome objections.

3. The third stage is to make decisions and reach an agreement.

Let's look at this process from the other person's perspective. Developing good relationships and getting results does not occur spontaneously. Consider what causes people to relate to us and follow our recommendations.

Trust

In developing a good relationship people must decide that we are some-one they can confide in and that our recommendations are for their ben-efit. Therefore, if we want people to open up to us and believe in what we say, we must convince them that they can *trust* us.

Think of how important relationships are in our lives, then realize that relationships are often gauged by the extent to which someone feels they can trust us. The more someone trusts us, the better the relationship.

Dependability

If we want people to assume that we are an authority and accept our ad-vice, then we must convince them that they can *depend* on us. If people are to feel comfortable following our instructions, then they need to re-spect us and believe they can rely on us. Realize how important results are in our lives and then recognize that results are only a by-product of how much people feel they can depend on us.

"I Care about You"

What causes people to trust us is when we assure them, "I care about you." Only when people feel we care about them will they trust us enough for us to establish rapport and develop good relationships.

In the famous Western Electric study of 1925, the industrial psychol-ogists wanted to determine the extent to which they could increase pro-duction by upgrading working conditions. They improved the lighting, and production increased. As they continued to improve lighting, pro-duction continued to rise. As a way of validating their study, the psy-chologists then reduced the lighting to discover to what extent produc-tion would decrease and were surprised to observe that production went even higher.

The correct conclusion was that the workers felt that management was interested in them. They could see people who seemed to be very con-cerned about them. The more attention they felt they were receiving, the more they believed that people cared about them.

From this day on, whenever we meet someone for the first time, we must realize that the person is asking us unconsciously and sponta-neously, "Are you someone who cares about me?" *The more we assure people that we care about them, the more they will trust us and thus the better the relationship.*

"I Can Take Care of You"

What causes people to feel they can depend on us is when we assure them "I can take care of you." If we want people to assume that we are an authority they can rely on to resolve their problems, then we want to assure them that we can take care of them. Only then will they depend on us. Then we can achieve our objectives and gain the desired results.

Warm and Sensitive

If we want people to believe that we care about them and in this way develop an ideal relationship, we need to project a certain type of personality. We should consider the qualities of those people who assure us that we can trust them and that we can believe that whatever they say is for our benefit. Such people are warm, sensitive, pleasant, caring, honest, sincere, kind, loving, compassionate, empathetic and friendly.

Aggressive and Dominant

Next we consider the strengths of those people who assure us that they can take care of us so that we feel comfortable depending on them and following their recommendations. Such people are confident, decisive, tough, forceful, resilient, persistent, dominant, reactive and aggressive.

Two Behavioral Patterns

Now evaluate which of these two personality types seems most like you:

Are you a warm, sensitive person who convinces people that you care about them so they can trust you? If so, you will easily establish rapport and create good relationships. However, if for fear of rejection you are not an aggressive, confident person, then people may not feel comfortable depending on you. For this reason, you may frequently wonder why, though you have developed good relationships, there are so few results to justify your efforts.

Correspondingly, if you are an aggressive, decisive person who quickly establishes a position of authority, then people may decide they can depend on you to take care of them. Therefore, they will follow your instructions, and you will gain good results. However, if for fear of appearing weak, you are not warm and sensitive, then people might question your sincerity. They may resent your success and believe that you are manipulative.

Developing Balance

If we can merge together the qualities of these two opposite personalities, then people will feel that we care about them and can also take care of them. People will, therefore, trust us and depend on us, and we will develop strong relationships and gain great results.

> If we keep our eye on the relationships, good results will usually follow.

Donald E. Petersen was the chairman of Ford Motor Co. from 1985 through 1990, when the company was particularly profitable. He explained his philosophy to Paul Ingrassia in a *Wall Street Journal* article: "Managing only for profits is like playing tennis with your eye on the scoreboard and not on the ball."

Baseball, also, provides a good analogy. Frequently the infielder is so anxious to throw to first base that he takes his eye off the ball. Likewise, salespeople are often so anxious to make quota that they press for the order before the prospect has all the information required. We must give people a chance to express their objections before we can expect to gain their agreement.

We need to know the score but always keep our mind focused on the relationship. We want to stay ambitious in achieving our objectives but first give attention to other people's needs. If we give them what they want, we will usually satisfy our needs.

Improving Our Performance

How might we change the way we perform and the impression we create? Do we need to become more sensitive so as to establish better relationships or more aggressive so we can get results?

We cannot be too aggressive, for this is a great quality; however, this personality trait can also become obnoxious. If our aggressiveness becomes abrasive, then we *do not* want to reduce this quality and avoid challenges. Rather *we enhance our aggressiveness with sensitivity*.

Equally, we cannot be too sensitive, for sensitivity is one of the most important personality qualities. However, sensitivity by itself can cause vulnerability. If we become too sensitive, then the solution is not to "chill out" or become cynical. Rather, we enhance our sensitivity with confidence, resiliency and inner strength.

We can never have too much of any one quality. If ever we have too much of a given quality, rather than reduce it, we can try to develop the opposite side instead. We enhance ourselves. We become aggressively sensitive.

Establishing rapport, understanding others' needs and developing solutions create the ideal relationship.

Creating a sense of urgency, resolving objections and seeking agreement assures results.

Becoming tenaciously pleasant creates the ideal balance.

25

The
Perfect
Child

We can achieve what we wish while gaining
the acceptance of others.

Children between the ages of one and four are perfect for four reasons. First, they are relentless. When they know what they want, they are eternally persistent. Second, they are proficient role players. They enjoy playing whatever role is necessary to gain the desired response as though stars in a Broadway show. They are spontaneous in their ability to relate to everyone so as to always get what they want. If we think about this ability, we may agree that it makes sense to rediscover our ability to relate to people if we want to succeed in business.

Third, they "shift gears at high speeds." They know how to sell. If one technique does not get them the chocolate chip cookie they want, then they move on to the next technique. More important than their ability to relate to people is their ability to keep trying new techniques until they find the combination of words that gets them what they want.

For a moment, focus on these last two qualities—relating to people and being able to sell effectively. Imagine we are remodeling a room in our home. We have been given the names of two contractors to evaluate.

The first person is someone we automatically like. We feel an instant rapport and are able to relate to this person. However, when we ask a question, the person uses terminology we do not understand and when we express an objection, the response is "Don't worry about it."

We do not dislike the second person, but there is no feeling of rapport. Yet when we ask a question, the person uses words we easily understand, and whenever we have an objection, we are given a thorough and sensible explanation.

Which person should we select? Should we prefer someone who establishes an ideal relationship with us or someone who clearly explains what we need? The idea is to develop the qualities of both of these people; one without the other will distract people. In today's competitive business environment we need both qualities.

To get back to children, we need to understand what makes them so successful at getting results. We cannot be upset by their relentless persistence, proficient role playing and high-speed gear shifting because they are so endearing. They are cheerful, amusing, friendly, witty, intelligent and brilliant—most of the time!

Young children especially are *professional hustlers.*

As an illustration, a child went to bed and, a moment later, called out, "Dad, can I have a glass of water?" His father replied, "You already had two glasses of water and one glass of juice, so get to sleep."

A moment later the child asked, "Dad, can I have a glass of water?" His father said, "If you don't get to sleep, I am going to spank you."

A few moments later, "Can I have a glass of water?" More angrily his father replied, "If you don't get to sleep, I will get a belt and spank you."

A moment later, "Dad, when you bring the belt, could you bring me a glass of water?"

What can we do in such a situation? We may have no choice but to give children what they are requesting, because their perseverance is also amusing and disarming.

Bringing Back Our Inherent Qualities

Possibly, as a child, we may have been persistent and relentless. Then, when we went to school, our teacher may have criticized us for speaking without permission. In embarrassment, we may have decided that we were no longer loved automatically for who we were but only if we performed or achieved according to someone else's expectations. Then we may have become inhibited. We may also notice people who speak only when spoken to and who have lost their spontaneity.

Are we as perfect today as we were at three years old? If not, what qualities have we lost? Maybe we can think back to a time when we were warm and sensitive and someone took advantage of our kindness or hurt our feelings. We may have decided that being warm and friendly were weaknesses and that while continuing to be aggressive we would no longer be as sympathetic or receptive as we once were.

If we have forgotten how perfect we were at three, then we need to watch children of that age. Most likely, we displayed some of their qualities of being relentless and charming when we were their age. Improving our personality in later life does not require developing new qualities as much as *rediscovering our inherent nature*. For us to succeed with people does *not* require changing our personality. What we need to do is get back some of those attributes of exuberance and persistence that we had as children. Which of the following do we need to become:

- More relentless in our persistence?

- More effective in our role playing?

- Better able to quickly change techniques?

- More disarming so that our persistence does not threaten people?

Disarming Negative People

Most of us avoid job responsibilities in which there is a considerable possibility of rejection. We may have difficulty pursuing our objectives if the rejection is more than we expected. Rita Pirrello has no problem with irritable people. Her viewpoint is one that we can all employ:

> My family owned a restaurant, and I began helping out at the age of eleven. When people are hungry, their personalities often change. They can become very irritable. If you understand why they are upset, then rather than taking it personally you decide it is only part of the job. The more you like your job, the more you will enjoy the challenge.

Rita has progressed through a variety of challenging jobs, working for a major bank, as a financial consultant for Shearson Lehman Brothers, and then as a training manager for them. Today, having married recently, Rita has returned to her hometown of Rockford, Illinois, and works as a broker, still for Shearson Lehman.

> The solution to rejection begins with our ability to know people. People are different. You need to develop a style within yourself that

is appropriate for each person and then have the flexibility to make the change. The chameleon survives and succeeds by adjusting to its environment. Our challenges might be more sophisticated, but our solutions are often as simple.

Rita is an identical twin. Her need for her own identity has fueled her competitiveness. Her desire to take care of people causes her to be sensitive, while her competitive spirit creates her resiliency. As her self-image is strengthened, she becomes more convinced that "the only reason why someone is rejecting me is because they don't know me. If we rationalize the rejection, there are no negative reactions or feelings."

Each of us develops ways of dealing with the stressful aspects of our life. What we do can help or retard the development of our potential. Rationalizing the problem can protect us from the unkindness of others. This protection can help us to persevere and become more productive, or it can help us to justify not making the effort. The choice is always ours. Rita believes "in being rewarded on our own merits":

> Therefore, we seek challenges that are reward-risk oriented. More important than becoming financially independent is to be exhilarated by challenges. Worse than failing, being rejected and experiencing anxiety is being bored. Whenever I become frustrated by the job, I ask myself why I joined the business. Then I take the challenge one step further. I take action to reduce the fear and take away the stress. Anxiety is created, not by what we do, but by what we avoid, so we need discipline. The greater the challenge and the greater the stress, the more we break the boredom.

The rewards we create balance the risks we confront.

Avoiding our responsibilities creates the anxiety that motivates us to discipline ourselves.

26
Staying on Target

> We must assure people that they can both trust and depend on us.

Selling the Presidency

The ability to gain people's trust, as well as make them feel comfortable depending on us, is best illustrated in the selling of the presidency. Newspapers and television examine every characteristic of the candidate. The slightest error is magnified and critically exposed.

> We balance our empathy with people with our decisiveness in taking care of them.

In 1972 the American public was forced to choose between two very opposite personalities. George McGovern was warm and sensitive. He assured us that he cared about us. Many felt they could trust him. However, McGovern was not an aggressive or decisive person. He frustrated his closest advisors with his inability to make a decision. Most

Americans felt he was someone who cared about them, but that he was not a strong personality who, in a crisis, could take care of them.

Richard Nixon convinced many with his aggressive determination that he could take care of us. Yet we also felt he did not care. We could depend on him to deal decisively with a crisis, but we worried that he was untrustworthy.

In the presidential election, however, when the American public was forced into a choice between extremes, they chose, by a landslide, someone they could depend on rather than someone to trust.

In a social gathering, we might prefer to be with a conversational person like George McGovern rather than someone like Richard Nixon, who might dominate the conversation. Nevertheless, when deciding between a presidential candidate we feel is a friend and a father figure, the father-type personality will usually get the vote.

Being Ambitiously Friendly

John F. Kennedy, in spite of his young age, minority religion and the notoriety of his father, was able to come from behind and win in 1960. He was considered one of the most charismatic presidents, and his death emotionally overwhelmed the American public. He was a very aggressive person, determined and ambitious, yet with warmth and humor so that people felt they could both trust and depend on him.

Ronald Reagan captured that same balance. On television he projected a strong, confident personality while disarming people with his smile and sense of humor.

In the summer of 1988 George Bush was seventeen points behind in the polls with a 40 percent negative rating. Bush was labeled a "wimp." The Doonesbury cartoon even showed President Reagan being asked, "Does George have any strengths?" and Reagan supposedly replied, "Yes, he never interrupts me." Suddenly, Bush became very aggressive, though Doonesbury claimed that it was not George who had made the personality change but his evil twin brother Skippy.

Bush may have had a true personality change, or possibly he was following the instructions of his campaign manager. Maybe he was recapturing his natural competitive spirit, evident when he played on the Yale University baseball team in the national championships two years in a row. All we know is that when Bush was in trouble, he had the ability to react and assure the American public that he could be decisive. He came from seventeen points behind to win by eight percentage points.

Many years ago a presidential candidate did not have to be charismatic to be elected. He would travel the country, speaking from the back of the train. The newspapers would print his speech, and the voters would usually make their decisions according to his policy regarding the issues.

Today elections are won and lost by the image the candidate projects on television news and debates. A primary factor in Jack Kennedy's election was Nixon's physical appearance during the television debates and the use of, or lack of, cosmetics.

Ronald Reagan was referred to as the "Teflon President." If he made a mistake, it did not stick. His ability as an actor was ideal for television. The challenge of selling the presidency is the same as any challenge in business. Today we often communicate through television, such as with videoconferencing and satellite television. We need to make a presentation that is dynamic and personable.

Our success in business is very much based on the impression we create. Our ability to assure people they can depend on us in a crisis can be more important than our intellectual abilities. We each need to evaluate how well we react under pressure. When we were children and we were loved automatically for who we were, then being persistent and disarming was easy. In the future if we can keep our balance, even when being rejected, we will gradually win people to our side.

Developing Balance

In the movie *Working Girl*, the heroine has high expectations. While she expects a great deal of herself, she is also a warm, sensitive person. Actually, she is so kind and receptive that people take advantage of her. While they trust her as a sincere and honest person, they do not give her any significant responsibility. Soon she becomes depressed and considers quitting.

She then takes on a position that does not belong to her and starts acting as though she is an authority. People assume that she is who she portrays herself to be and begin to respect her. As they start depending on her, she begins to succeed. Her success soon reinforces her new self-image, making her confidence real.

This can be one of the most natural ways of developing our potential. We play the role and keep making corrections until we gain the desired response. Then we *integrate the positive feedback into our self-image* and strengthen our sense of identity.

Capitalizing on Negative Feedback

Steve Alper is part of Shearson Lehman Brothers' training program, helping their financial consultants to succeed in a stressful, risk-oriented business. When Steve was in college, he did telemarketing for a publishing company. His job was not in sales but research. People were rarely returning his phone calls.

Finally he decided,

I've got to turn this around. I don't like failing. I made an adjustment in my approach and immediately began to succeed.We constantly need to reevaluate and improve on our techniques for dealing with people. Reaching a peak performance is based on maintaining a positive leverage in an environment that many people perceive to be negative. When you decide that it is always a learning environment, then there are no obstacles. Treating people like dollar signs will negatively affect the relationships. Their rejection, which is understandable, will soon cause you to become defensive. Instead we must decide that rejection, rather than being an obstacle, does not exist. It is just a feedback device for making adjustments in the way we think about people and, therefore, how we treat them.

> Rejection provides the data we need to make
> the necessary adjustments.

If you always succeeded, then there would be no anticipation, and the job would no longer be fun. For me the failures and rejections become all the same. They are both data. Just make the adjustments. Of course, *the best adjustment is the anticipation of the problem.* The forethought prepares you for any possible obstacles and objections. As a college professor taught me, "If your plan fails it's because you failed to plan."

Steve keeps himself focused on three words: confidence, attitude and discipline. *Having inner confidence creates the positive attitude that keeps us disciplined.* We can begin the cycle with any of these three words. Change our attitude and we become disciplined and create the success that gives us the confidence that justifies the attitude.

Making the Necessary Adjustments

As an illustration, the modern torpedo first *decides which target* it wants to reach. Second, it *sends out signals*. Then the torpedo has *a sensing device to receive feedback* so that it knows if it is off course or on target. Finally, if the feedback is negative, the torpedo has *the ability to make course corrections* to get back on target.

Now imagine a torpedo that has an ego and takes it personally every time it gets negative feedback. What will the torpedo do?

It might go around in circles, waiting for positive signals. Many of us function in the same way. We try protecting ourselves from any further negative feedback, which we assume to be rejection, by procrastinating. We might do paperwork or become involved in non-productive activities. Each of us needs to think of how often we are caught in this protective cycle.

Another negative option for the torpedo is to go to the bottom, as some of us frequently do when we feel overwhelmed. We actually quit, or at least we disappear for a while. We might call in sick and stay home. Maybe we sleep late and watch television rather than dealing with confrontation.

The torpedo may go back home, which would be disastrous to the submarine. Yet in business that is often what we do. Some of us even go back home and have our spouse support us, at least temporarily.

The torpedo might get overheated by taking the negative feedback too personally and blow up. Unfortunately we are all vulnerable to this possibility. If we blow up externally, we become angry. We might yell at a secretary or become abusive with our family when we get home. If we blow up internally, then the problem might be suicide, overdosing on drugs or depending on alcohol.

Another negative option for the torpedo is to continue on its original course, oblivious to the feedback, miss the target and only hit another by accident. We often react with the same pattern. We disregard any negative feedback and just keep on moving. In selling, if the prospect hangs up, we make our next call. If we have enough targets, then by merely playing the percentages we will hit one. Yet we might miss many opportunities.

Just like the modern torpedo, we can also enjoy negative feedback. Our ego, which is our sensing device, is sensitive, but is not oversensitive. We want to *monitor* the negative feedback and *modify* our approach to keep moving in the right direction, until we reach our objective. In other words, *we appreciate the negative feedback as the information we need to reach our target*.

Feel, Felt, Found

Walt Wiesenhutter today is succeeding in his own business, enjoying his independence and the challenge of marketing. His success was forced upon him. He told me his story:

> I lost my job after twenty-two years. My company was taken over, and my seniority and performance meant nothing to the new managers. I tried as best I could to minimize the feelings of rejection. Your value as a person is damaged. Even though you internalize the rejection and bad feelings, you can also find inner strength. Failure is positive when you allow it to change your priorities and move forward.

One way of capitalizing on negative feedback is when we use the technique referred to as "feel, felt, found." When someone disagrees with us, rather than arguing, we should say instead: "I know how you *feel*. I once *felt* the same myself. However, because of my experience in such situations, I have *found* if we do it this way in advance, the problem is solved before it occurs."

For example, a man received a call from his wife telling him that his son's turtle had died and that he should come home early and console him.

When the father arrived home, he was prepared. He said to his son, "I know just how you *feel*. I once *felt* the same myself, when my pet canary died. However, because of this experience, I have *found* that if we find a pretty place in the backyard for your turtle, have your friends over for some hymns and prayers, and then have cake and ice cream, you will feel better."

His son seemed happier as they built a little coffin and dug a tiny grave. Then Dad said, "Johnny, in preparation for your friends' arrival, get the turtle." So Johnny brought the turtle to his father. But when he handed the turtle to his father, the turtle moved, and his Dad said, "Look, Johnny, your turtle is still alive."

And Johnny said, "Daddy, let's kill it."

Negative feedback provides the information we need to stay on target.

We gain acceptance by caring about people.

People respect us when we assure them
that we can take care of them.

We project the image that creates the desired response,
which strengthens our identity.

Monitoring others' feelings helps us understand
the ways we need to modify our approach.

We develop an attitude of confidence, which creates self-discipline.

3

Anxiety, A Source of Creative Energy

27
Succeeding under Stress

> The more we are stimulated by stress, the more we will enjoy challenging ourselves.

Until this century there were few causes of stress. Many Americans lived on the farm, where there was no rush hour traffic, checkbooks to balance or confined work spaces. Whatever stress we experienced was quickly relieved by the physical demands of living. Milking cows, tilling the soil and preparing food are all natural expenditures of anxious energy.

An Age of Anxiety

In the commercial enterprises of today, however, there are many causes of frustration and tension. At work we often have to accept the authority of people we might not like. A major part of our day might be wasted in stop-and-go traffic that we cannot avoid. We may experience a loss of freedom when working in a bureaucratic, corporate environment.

An even more serious problem of modern society is that we have so few ways to reduce tension. We have to smile at people who offend us rather than express any anger we feel. We have to drive carefully when we are anxious to get home or get one more ticket and risk losing our license.

When we leave the solitude and relative isolation of the farm and move to a crowded city, this tension escalates. The healthy physical exhaustion of the farm is replaced by violence, such as gunfire on Los Angeles freeways. Advertisements encourage us to smoke, drink alcoholic beverages and eat junk food. People encourage us to use illicit drugs. Gambling can exhaust our financial resources.

The switch from a life-style that included relatively few causes of stress and many natural ways of productively easing tension to a society in which we easily become upset with few ways of dealing with the anxiety brings a personal challenge. We either learn how stress can stimulate and exhilarate us or we are overwhelmed by emotional pressures.

Robert Hoffman is a nationally recognized medical authority in the clinical application of behavioral medicine and a student of the rapidly emerging field of psychoneuroimmunology. He lectures internationally and recently returned from England where he was a visiting professor. He suggests the following:

> Stress is an inevitable part of life. There is no way to be alive and avoid anxiety altogether. Stress is not bad. It can challenge an individual to achieve mastery....Accomplishments represent triumphs over stress.
>
> However, all people have windows of vulnerability, areas of inability to manage certain kinds of stress successfully. All human beings develop character armor during their formative years, which essentially represents stress management styles, that is, patterns of behavior for handling stress. Some weakness, when subjected to stress, leads to distress, even "dis-ease," of the body, mind or both.
>
> Accumulating scientific research from both animal and human studies suggests that the kinds of stress that produce learned helplessness cause suppression of the body's natural defenses against disease and, therefore, render the organism more susceptible to the development of illness.

> Adversity is a call to arms.

Conversely, empowerment correlates with immuno enhancement, and improved survival. Simply put, those who allow themselves to become chronic victims are more likely to suffer breakdown and less likely to overcome adversity. Behavioral techniques that empower will strengthen those who employ them.

Environmental Conditioning

We tend to adapt to our environment. If our parents go to church, drink martinis and play golf, we may conform to their way of living, or we may decide to use illegal drugs, oversleep and play pool.

For a moment we need to stop reacting and start thinking of what makes sense. We need to stop being a product of our environment and begin to create an environment that is healthy, rewarding and meaningful.

Think of the causes of our frustration, such as crowds, loud noises and a rigidly structured environment. Now consider those activities that relax us but are nonproductive, such as watching television or overeating. What we want to incorporate in our lives are productive activities that are relaxing and dissipate stress, like taking a walk at sunset, reading a book by a fireplace or having a conversation with a friend.

Taking Control

Bob Dobry was working for a company and feeling frustrated that he was not in control of his life. Then he reviewed those activities he most enjoyed. They included flying, marketing and being in contact with people. The result of this self-evaluation was his own aerial advertising business. Now his favorite activities and his business have become synonymous. Flying, making money, having control of his destiny and satisfying his clients' needs have become one and the same.

People who own their businesses may have more control over their lives but also more frustration. Prospects might be negative and anxiety increase. Bob described the situation to me:

When you are overloaded from being rejected, the stress often immobilizes you. Once you are inundated, you want to sleep or watch television. In that moment you need to take positive action.

The secret to winning is deciding that all you are doing is playing a game. I remind myself that by living life on the lighter side the negatives become easier to accept. You can continue on rather than feeling suffocated and losing your energy.

Changing our perception can disengage the stress.

Failure is only a happening. Last week I made eighteen calls in one morning. Half were positive; they agreed to receive my media kit, and two made appointments. The negatives were not negative but only steps toward what I really wanted. It's refreshing to learn that rejection and stress should be welcomed as long as we convert the experience into a benefit.

Failure and rejection are only a problem when they cause us to feel bad. If disappointment and negative feedback cause excessive stress, we may become defensive. Negative experiences can be dangerous if they cause negative energy.

If we ever again take failure and rejection personally, then we have one last chance to succeed. We need to develop positive reactions toward the anxiety which the adversity and negative feedback are creating within us.

A crisis can be the best time for growth.

The year 1970 was a turning point for Elson Lui, who at that time was a computer engineer. His training was technical. He was good at problem solving and details. His personality was analytical, rational and deliberate, but he wanted to develop his potential and expand his opportunities. He decided that selling for his company could be the solution, but they told him he lacked the necessary qualities.

Elson decided to test his ability by selling insurance on a part-time basis. His success convinced him to begin a full-time career in marketing, and within a year he had placed first in his new company and won a trip to Rome. He was then transferred to Hong Kong. He sold all his furniture and his home, and then, as he was ready to fly to Asia, the company's Hong Kong operation collapsed. He shared his experience:

> It was a disaster. Only my positive thoughts kept me moving in the right direction. I kept reminding myself that being in the middle of catastrophe is the best time for personal growth. I convinced myself that a positive surprise was waiting around the corner. I also began to share my ideas. Teaching crystallizes your own thoughts and internalizes positive attitudes.

Elson researched the economic opportunities. People were worried about the economy and investing in precious metals. Within six months he sold over $1 million in gold and silver.

> Then a divorce wiped me out, and my wife received the business. When you are in a crisis, you have to relax, go within yourself and ask your creativity to give you insight. Your creativity comes in the quiet times. You get clear during this valuable period. You can focus

your strengths and weaknesses. You also can understand where you have been diverted off the track.

> **Tension creates ego strength.**

Stress can distract our view of reality. We can lose sight of our opportunities and our own abilities. In the past, if I was upset, I would keep it inside rather than having an argument. I no longer worry so much about what others think of me as to feel hurt, but instead think of how their feelings can help me to become more creative and productive. Stress can bring our view of reality more clearly into focus.

When you work out in the gym, such as at the bench press, your muscles need to be under pressure to build strength. We all need to use tension to make ourselves better rather than avoid the pain, whether in developing muscle strength or ego strength. You allow the negative forces to defeat you, or you defeat them by making the stress and discomfort work for you.

Failure and rejection can generate emotional pressure that hinders or propels us to succeed in business. We need the courage to understand our vulnerabilities. Elson went on to explain:

Negative feedback can help you focus on people, recognize the differences in people and make the necessary adjustments. Once they can relate to you, then your fears of rejection are resolved. We need to be critical of ourselves if we are going to make important changes in our self-image. This process depends on where we are within the spectrum of being warm and sensitive to aggressive and dominant. Then we need to move the pendulum.

Life can be very stressful. Yet, if we allow stress to stimulate us, we can more easily achieve our objectives. Recognize the direct relationship between our ability to capitalize on stress and our effectiveness in developing our potential.

> **The simplest way to eliminate stress is to decide there is no problem.**

28
Benefits
of Anxiety

> Stress is energy that can keep us in continuous movement
> until we reach our objective.

Before discussing the two primary benefits of anxiety, we should appreciate how every part of our world can provide benefit. In other words, all we experience, including pain, is a gift. If we are unable to experience pain, we might damage ourselves and never know we were hurt.

Isolating Our Vulnerability

So pain has value, for it tells us that we are moving in the wrong direction. Though pain does not feel good, it is a signal to pay attention. Pain is asking us to stop what we are doing and determine what is hurting us. Anxiety provides the same opportunity. Anxiety is psychological pain. It is asking us to stop what we are doing and determine the origins of our frustration. The primary reason we become upset is because there is a vulnerability within us that has yet to be resolved. Anxiety therefore helps us *isolate our vulnerability*. This becomes the first benefit of anxiety.

Some problems upset up because they are petty, such as paperwork or cleaning the garage. Other challenges excite us, such as sailing or making a presentation in business. Then there might be responsibilities such as dealing with aggressive people where we feel vulnerable.

We are presented with three kinds of situations:

1. Petty situations, which we feel are beneath our self-image
2. Difficult situations, which threaten our self-image
3. Ideal situations, which we enjoy because they challenge and stimulate us without overwhelming us

From this day on, whenever we are frustrated, we need to think back to when we felt good. Next we remember when we became frustrated and what happened to upset us. We want to isolate the moment in which the anxiety began. Then we remind ourselves that what occurred was a catalyst which triggered a vulnerability within us.

Of course, our frustrations are often the result of a succession of events. The frequency of the problems eventually creates a "last straw" situation. The sooner we can objectively take control of the process, the more quickly we position ourselves to break the negative chain reaction.

Once we have determined the cause of our anxiety, we can then apply either of two solutions. One is to *release* the problem, and the other is to *confront* it. The two factors that determine which solution to use is whether the problem is minor or of substance. If the problem is minor, then we release it. If our problem is substantial, we deal with and confront it.

I met Mark Victor Hansen when I was giving a lecture in New York City in 1973. A year later Mark went bankrupt. The oil crisis eliminated the supplies he needed for his manufacturing company, and he lost $2 million in one day. He related the story to me:

It was like a wake-up call. Ever since then my bad times have become my good times, and my worst experiences have become my best experiences. When you are inside the disaster, you often can't see a way out. Only over a period of time can you become thankful of what has happened. In retrospect, we appreciate what we have gained.

Today Mark gives seminars in which he helps people see where they are, imagine where they want to be and visualize the way to succeed. His word pictures help people to enhance their imaginative skills. He explained how we need to ask for outside help:

Often we feel as though we are in a quagmire and the situation seems near impossible. Then only our objectivity can pull us out. There are so many ways in which we can quicken the objectivity and become thankful sooner. One is by asking someone who is on the outside and can see through our blind spots.

When we experience adversity we need to recycle ourselves as a way of finding our purpose. We are only lazy when we have yet to find what is right for us. When we find our purpose, then every problem has value. Our perspective makes all the difference. When we find the value in bad experiences, we stimulate our mental resources.

Everyone gets hit, financially and emotionally, and when the difficult times begin, we need to drink in all the positives. Having a positive cohort who is on the other side can keep us mobilized in purposeful action. We need people who can inspire us.

Developing Inner Strength

We might fail, but if people still love us, we can still feel good. Succeeding in business today requires inner strength, which is not easily developed. There are techniques, however, that can speed up the process:

- Make one change per day, regardless of how small, that promotes progress.

- Ask for advice from someone we respect and incorporate that person's suggestion(s) into our own strategies.

- Try a new approach, such as driving home a different way or developing new skills that might enhance our jobs.

- Study another culture, specifically the way they deal with stress.

Mark discussed one of the most significant and meaningful moments in his life—A Japanese funeral:

> You write your feelings for the one who has died, whether feelings of love or hate. Then everyone puts their notes into a paper boat that is floating on the water. The boat is then set on fire, and any hate then burns away, so there are no bad feelings lingering within us. When people are unkind to us, we need to write down how we feel. Then put the paper away for three days, pull it out and read the words. Then we need to release the feelings by burning the paper.
>
> Everyone gets rejected. Too often we only feel our own pain. We need to know that everyone goes through these negative feelings. It's universal. We feel rejected when the negative feedback is saying, "I am not enough." We need to remind ourselves, "I am enough."

In the end our satisfaction depends not on what happens but on how we feel about what happens. Mark believes we need "to resolve the anxiety without malice." He keeps audiocassettes of his four favorite comedians in his car. He exercises consistently. He believes that passion transcends the petty irritation and keeps us in a positive momentum.

Think of the effect that music has on our mood. I can be irritated and, by listening to certain parts of the sound track from the movie *The Mission,* feel completely calm and at peace with the world. I can be depressed and, after a few minutes of the music from *Star Wars,* feel emotionally ready to take on my next challenge.

We all have to wonder how serious our problems might be when merely by listening to the appropriate music our emotions can change so quickly. Often I prefer to stay upset rather than listen to music that will quickly make me feel good. Instead, I want to work through the problem rather than experience a "quick fix." I want to understand why I am taking the situation so seriously. Then I decide whether it is petty and I should release the frustration or if the problem is of substance and needs to be confronted.

Too often we worry about situations that are insignificant. We need to think of how often we worry about possible problems that never occur. We may realize that more than half of what we worry about never occurs.

Too often we worry about what is meaningless and disregard the serious situations of our lives. There are those of us, for example, who live for soap operas or sporting events while neglecting our health, our work or our family. We have to be amused by those who actually write hate mail to television soap opera actors or actresses, as though the program and the characters were real. Equally, there are some of us whose happiness rises and falls with the success or failure of a football team, while we are out of shape, avoid business responsibilities and disregard our families.

Confront what is of substance and release what is petty.

Take a Realistic View

There is a tale of two people who were to be married. The groom was visiting the bride's family for the first time, when she went to the basement to get potatoes but never returned. Her father went to the basement to determine the problem, and he never returned. Her mother went to find them, and the young man was now alone.

Then he went to the basement, only to find them crying. He asked his fiancée what the problem was and she showed him an ax in the ceiling and, while continuing to cry, explained to him, "When we are married and have a child, our child will come down here to play, and the ax might fall from the ceiling and kill our child."

So he said, "Then why don't we just remove the ax from the ceiling?"

Whenever we have a problem, we can choose from three solutions:

1. Remove the ax from the ceiling and solve the problem
2. Disregard the problem because it is not worth our effort
3. Take the self defeating approach, which is to sit around and cry about it.

We all need to remember the prayer of serenity:

> God grant me the serenity to accept the things I cannot change, courage to change the things I can and wisdom to know the difference.

Energy for Continuous Movement

Anxiety is energy that is toxic only if internalized. If we keep the stress within us, it will promote self-destructive behavior. We may become depressed and defensive or hostile and abusive. However, when the anxiety is used instead as a stimulus for achievement, it can power us through the obstacles many of us avoid. Therefore, the second benefit of anxiety is as *energy for continuous movement*.

As an illustration, consider animals that are predators and those which are preyed upon. There is one factor that distinguishes predators from their prey, and that is the position of their eyes. The hunted have eyes on the sides of their heads. Their peripheral vision is for survival purposes. They can look in all directions as they nervously watch for predators. Notice that size is not a factor, for this group includes big animals, such as elk, horses and cows, and small animals, such as mice, rabbits and squirrels.

Hunters have eyes that look straight ahead, such as wolves, coyotes, lions, tigers and people. We might not like the idea that we are physiologically and instinctively conditioned to enjoy the hunt. However, we need to accept this inherent part of our nature if we are to understand why we experience anxiety so easily. Turtles experience very little stress. Cows and sheep are also relaxed animals. Yet predators can quickly become irritable when their needs are not being satisfied.

Recognize how we deal with stress. Too often we keep the anxiety inside ourselves, which causes depression and feelings of despair. Such negative energy can motivate us to avoid any further challenges, for fear of further frustration. Instead we need to convert the anxiety into some form of activity that enhances our self-image. We want to reduce the valleys where we are emotionally down and increase the frequency of feeling as though we are on top of a mountain. We do both when we *channel anxiety into a force for achievement.*

As an example, the male aborigine in Australia today still hunts the kangaroo as he has for thousands of years. At dawn he takes up the hunt and chases the kangaroo. He cannot catch it but pursues it all day long. When darkness comes and he has no idea where the kangaroo has gone, he falls asleep. The kangaroo, realizing it is no longer being hunted, soon stops and falls asleep.

The next morning, at sunrise, the aborigine resumes the hunt. The kangaroo hears him coming and attempts to start running again but has difficulty moving. It has not previously had to run an entire day as it did the day before. Its ligaments, cartilage and muscle have stiffened up. It is unable to take flight. The aborigine continues moving steadily, kills the kangaroo and carries it back.

Our instinct is to be continuously on the move until we have channeled the anxiety into activities that produce the desired results. For this reason, next time we are in a social gathering and someone asks us what kind of work we do, we should be honest and tell them, "I'm a hunter and gatherer." When we become frustrated, we do not keep the anxiety inside of ourselves and become depressed. We return to our inherent nature by converting stress into productive energy.

A problem has two parts: the problem itself and the anxiety that the problem creates. Therefore, if we can eliminate the problem before it causes anxiety, we are protecting ourselves from becoming depressed or hostile. However, if an awareness of our vulnerabilities does not solve the problem, then we must learn how to channel the anxiety into creative and productive energy.

The Anxiety Cycle

The energy created by anxiety can be expressed in three ways: through depression that causes immobility, hostility that results in over-reactive behavior and creativity that sharpens our objectivity. Initially anxiety is within us, which causes us to be depressed. Depression might be the most serious problem in our society.

Think of why we become depressed as deeply, as often and as long as we do. Maybe we are afraid of expressing our frustrations outwardly for fear we might antagonize someone. The person may no longer like us, causing us more anxiety which can result in deeper depression. For this reason many of us keep the anxiety within ourselves for fear that if we try releasing our negative feelings we might only compound the problem.

Some of us do not believe in being frustrated. Rather than experience insomnia, hypertension or ulcers, we give other people ulcers. We are carriers who believe in sharing our frustrations. Instead of being depressed, we express our anxiety outwardly and become angry.

We need to develop creative ways of releasing our frustrations. We want to stay depressed only long enough to determine why we are upset. Then we need to resolve the conflict and move on.

Expressing Anger Creatively

We cannot be so afraid of becoming angry as to keep the anxiety within ourselves. When we channel our frustration outward, we may irritate people. However, if we keep expressing ourselves intelligently, humorously and sensibly, we will soon develop a repertoire of ways to creatively eliminate anxiety.

We can channel our frustration into activities that give us a sense of achievement. We may also discover that humor is an emotionally healthy way of dealing with situations that would otherwise cause us to become depressed or angry.

Dick Gregory, today an activist, was a successful comedian in the sixties. He once bought an expensive home in a wealthy section of Chicago. It was summertime, and his neighbors were on vacation.

A week later, Dick was mowing the grass when his neighbors returned. The man of the house walked across the lawn and asked him, "Hey, boy, what do you get for mowing the lawn?" and Dick said, "I get to sleep with the lady inside." He could have become upset by the implication of the question and felt depressed or angry. Instead he used his intelligence to be humorous and creative.

Humor is inherently creative. Sometimes we need to see the world, not as it is, but as we wish it to be. Then we can think of how to transform the frustrations of our disappointment into an amusement, so that the tension is released. Soon conflict and stress is replaced by harmony, and everyone feels better.

When people frustrate us, we need to be imaginative in developing an approach that is clever, charming, and creative. A frustrating incident becomes our opportunity to develop our sense of humor.

> Frustration is our early warning signal.

Anxiety isolates our vulnerability so we know
when and where change needs to occur.

We release the problem if it is petty and confront it
if it is of substance.

29
Negative
Addictions

> Happiness is based on modifying our expectations
> to keep ourselves in balance.

Most of us do not enjoy stress. Being under emotional pressure is no fun. When we experience toxic energy such as feeling tense or anxious, we will seek devices to relieve us of the irritation. If the device effectively eliminates tension, we might then become so dependent on the technique as to be addicted.

There are ten self-destructive addictions that we use to cope with stress. These addictions can hurt our health, reduce longevity, neutralize our energy, decrease our endurance and vitality, create a negative impact on people, cut us off from reality, stifle creativity, damage our self-image and reduce self-esteem, as well as our results in life.

In the next chapter we will discuss the four positive addictions for dealing with anxiety. These positive addictions do not help us to cope with stress. The word *cope* is too ineffective. They cause us to *thrive* on stress. They give us a sense of achievement, help us confront reality and improve our impact on people. They increase our energy, endurance, longevity and vitality, while improving our health. They sharpen our creativity, enhance our self-image and increase self-esteem, as well as our results in life.

The ten negative addictions are

Smoking	Oversleeping
Alcohol	Drugs
Caffeine	Gambling
Food	Depression
Television	Hostility

Recognize that all negatives are either "uppers" or "downers." They either raise our energy or tranquilize us.

> **We must challenge ourselves when we are bored and be easy on ourselves when we feel overwhelmed.**

Also realize that there are only two causes of stress: *boredom* when we feel a lack of challenge and *burnout* when our challenges overwhelm us. They are both caused by our expectations. If our expectations are unreasonably high, then we are vulnerable to burnout. In other words, we are in danger of overload and short circuiting. If our expectations are too low, our vulnerability could be boredom. Therefore, *happiness is based on modifying our expectations to keep ourselves in balance.*

Stimulated and Mellow

Consider the two emotions that we do want to experience: to be *stimulated*, such as being turned on and excited, and *mellow*, such as being comfortable, relaxed and content.

We want to raise our expectations in order to be stimulated. However, if we demand too much of ourselves we might be in danger of burnout. Then, we need to lower our expectations, such as taking a long weekend, reading a book and being mellow. Yet, if we become too relaxed, we might be in danger of boredom. Therefore, we need to enjoy the highs of being stimulated and the lows of being mellow while avoiding the boredom and burnout reactions.

Those of us who hate boredom and need to be stimulated will often self-destructively depend on uppers. Many of us enjoy being hyper and love crisis. The danger that we might "wipe out" creates an "adrenaline high." We purposely create stress to feel a sense of excitement in our lives.

Then there are those of us who want to tranquilize and pacify our mind, body and ego. We are in danger of self-destructively depending on downers to avoid the pressure of our own responsibilities. We tend to be oversensitive, vulnerable and avoid confrontation.

Take a look at the ten negative addictions and score them as uppers or downers. Notice that two are both uppers and downers. Then identify which of these negatives, if any, you most depend on. Dependence on uppers indicates that you hate boredom and enjoy experiencing an adrenal high. Dependence on downers implies that your expectations are motivating you into such stressful situations that you want to pacify your ego in order to survive emotionally.

Smoking is an upper. Nicotine constricts the blood vessels, which reduces the flow of oxygen to the brain. The brain, depleted of oxygen, sends a message to our adrenal glands to release adrenaline into the heart to increase the flow of blood so as to compensate for the depletion of oxygen. The heart is now beating, on the average, 22 percent faster than usual. Smoking is therefore an upper for those of us who hate depression, cannot tolerate mental fatigue and find in a single cigarette the equivalent of a fast shot of adrenaline. Thus tobacco is a stimulant.

Alcohol is a downer. Alcohol is not a relaxant but a depressant. Drinking is for those of us who want to tranquilize our ego from reality. The reason some of us think it is an upper is because alcohol can bring us down below our inhibitors so that we no longer care what the reactions of others might be. We become spontaneous and perhaps express our fears and anger or tell silly stories. Again, such reactions occur only because we have become so relaxed and lacking in control that we do not care what others think of us.

Caffeine is an upper. Many of us depend on coffee to get ourselves started in the morning and keep ourselves alert throughout the day, as well as at night. Yet caffeine does not give us any energy. The reason why coffee stimulates us is because it is a drug. However, while exciting us, it also depletes energy and causes a letdown afterwards. Caffeine also precipitates hyperactive reactions, increasing the heart beat, and disrupting the time clocks in our physiological system, such as eating and sleep cycles. In addition, it is a factor in the onset of panic attacks among 15 percent of the population, while causing nervousness in almost everyone.

Those of us who drink caffeine beverages but do not believe we are addicted to caffeine should experiment by avoiding it for a few days. We may experience a variety of withdrawal reactions, such as having difficulty awakening in the morning or staying awake throughout the day, as well as the occurrence of frequent headaches.

Food is both an upper and a downer. Sugar that is processed by machines, refined and ready to be digested immediately, is an upper.

Refined sugar requires an insulin reaction, which quickly, though temporarily, gives us a fast high. Downer-type foods take hours to digest, causing us to become groggy, sleepy and sluggish. These are fat and protein, such as meat, eggs, cheese, whole milk, creams, sauces, butter and ice cream.

Our ideal diet is complex carbohydrates, which include natural grains, vegetables and fruit. These foods have two important ingredients. One is fiber, which our body processes in a way that causes our mind to stay alert and our body to be cleansed. The second is complex sugar, in which the molecules break down slowly, giving us steady energy. This is the reason why, if we go to a Chinese restaurant and stuff ourselves on rice and vegetables, we may walk out thinking to ourselves, "I feel like I didn't eat," because we do not feel full.

Think of the relationship between food and stress. We often deal with stress by eating those foods that give us the reaction we desire. If we want to eliminate feelings of depression, then foods with refined sugar will stimulate us by creating a quick upper reaction. Correspondingly, if we are experiencing too much stress and we want to relax, then the downer type of foods pacify us, causing us to feel tranquilized. We need to understand the relationship between stress, addictions and our success.

Television is a downer. Watching the same station for just thirty seconds significantly reduces the electrical brain wave level frequencies, causing our mind to become mesmerized, often for hours. Research, though not well documented, indicates that television may cause atrophy of the dendrites on the brain cells. Television may also be the most passive activity.

Oversleep is a downer. Any adult who sleeps more than seven or eight hours per night is probably using sleep as an escape from reality. By purposefully oversleeping we avoid responsibilities that we do not want to confront. Oversleep can also cause headaches.

Drugs can be both uppers and downers. Cocaine, LSD, other psychedelic drugs and amphetamines are stimulants. Downers would be such tranquilizers as Valium, barbiturates and marijuana. We do not need tranquilizers to dull the edges of our lives.

The type of drug that we become addicted to is an indication of the cause of our frustration. Being addicted to uppers indicates someone who becomes bored easily and feels a need to be stimulated. Those who depend on downers probably have difficulty with reality, experience too much stress and want to tranquilize themselves.

Gambling and spending money are uppers. Depression sets in later when we run out of money.

Depression is an obvious downer in which we have a conditioned reaction to internalized stress. This manifests itself in such avoidance behavior as procrastination, lethargy and crying.

Many of us have a conditioned reaction to externalize stress and become violent or abusive. Hostility, manifesting itself in starting arguments and irritating people just to amuse ourselves, is an upper.

Moving Away from Addiction

> The first step to eliminating a negative addiction is admitting our dependency.

Jack Rux, after a successful sales career in the high technology arena, has become a sales and marketing consultant. Along the way he has had a few stressful experiences, which have convinced him that "as we mature, we are able to share our failures as well as our successes." As with many of us, Jack had high expectations, but did not really know which path to take. He decided that becoming a pharmacist would be satisfying professionally, so he earned his masters degree. Then he discovered that he hated the work:

> My distaste was so strong that I became depressed. I would go to sleep at sunset and sleep till sunrise and with twelve hours of sleep still be tired. Then the doctors put me on enough Valium to turn me into a zombie, all because I hated my job. I was twenty-six years old, and I felt I had no future.
>
> I had a choice: stay miserable and depressed or make the toughest decision of my life. It is hard to imagine how scary it was to drop my career, throw away seven years of hard work and my degree and start over. I had spent my life doing what was right for everyone else. It was time to do something for me. But I had no skills, expertise or experience. The only solution I could think of was to go into sales.
>
> I also decided, as frightened as I was, that there was no way I could tolerate another failure. Unknowingly I had jumped into a profession that is filled with failure and rejection. There I was, psychologically crippled, full of fear and totally unsure of myself. I was the least likely candidate to succeed, but I succeeded beyond my wildest expectations.

Jack's success began in the same way as everyone else's who succeeds. He made a decision. Jack decided to make "a commitment to take control of my life":

I took full responsibility for everything I did. If something had happened, it was my fault. My success was assured. My business was booming, and I accumulated enough money to pay off all my debts, buy a wonderful house and have money left over for exotic vacations.

> **Success positions us for greater opportunity as well as the danger of losing what we already have gained.**

The more someone succeeds, the more they are in danger of developing the "King Midas touch complex." From mythology we remember that King Midas wished that whatever he touched would turn to gold. *Be very careful what you wish for in life, for you may receive it and discover it was not what you wanted.* Whatever King Midas touched turned to gold, including his wife, children and food. Many of us, when we succeed, also develop the false assumption that whatever we touch will turn to gold.

> **Success can blind us to the danger built into our opportunities.**

Jack continues his story:

I then made a mistake. I played "Bet the Company." The opportunity to expand my firm was too tempting. Sure there were risks, but I always took risks. Risk taking was my way of life, and if I were right, I would become an overnight millionaire.

I was wrong. Blinded by the potential profits, in eleven months I went from successful entrepreneur with money in the bank to flat broke. And I mean broke.

Being broke is frightening. All your hopes and dreams are lost in the emotions of fending off creditors. Your self-esteem drops to an all-time low. The embarrassment of potential bankruptcy makes you avoid old friends, and it seems no one cares. Your world has come to an end. I had sold off everything of value to finance my money-gobbling decision. The business was dead, and I was hopelessly in debt. Perhaps it was pride, but I never was able to file for bankruptcy. It was the logical decision, but somehow I just couldn't walk away from my obligations.

Self-Analysis at the Crossroads

I asked myself, "Why do some of us prevail and become stronger, while others collapse under the weight of the hardship? What separates the achiever from the also-ran?

You must view yourself as capable of becoming successful. Until you decide that you can be successful, until you make the choice to be successful, your efforts will be futile. You must develop the perseverance to continue your journey no matter what obstacles may get in the way. If you haven't made the decision to be successful, if you don't view yourself as a success, the roadblocks will stop you cold.

Self-Image and Stress

What does it say about our self-image if we are still depending on negative addictions? Obviously, we are not thinking very highly of ourselves. *The more positive our self-image, the more we are willing to suffer through physical and emotional pain to drop negatives and add positives.*

Many years ago my older son, when he completed college and returned home, would party and drink beer on Friday night. He would sleep until early afternoon on Saturday, sleep late on Sunday morning and be groggy on Monday. I expressed my concern that he might have a drinking problem. He said, "If I can drink twelve beers on Friday night, then how can I have a problem?"

As he continued in this pattern, my daughter Michelle said to him, "Dad says each of us has a child within us, and we have to be good to our child. Are you being good to your child?" Arthur then joined AA and has been sober for years. Whether the addiction is drugs, alcohol, smoking or compulsive eating, we need to take care of our inner child. We should want to be kind to ourselves.

> The causes of stress are boredom and burnout.

> We must raise our expectations when we are bored, and we must become more patient with ourselves when we are experiencing burnout.

> The stronger our self-image, the more easily we will eliminate negative addictions.

30
Positive Addictions

> Anxiety-eliminating techniques are positive when they relieve stress while also increasing our results.

Exercise

The first positive addiction is exercise, particularly an aerobic sport such as jogging, swimming, cycling, brisk walking, rowing, canoeing, aerobic dancing, cross-country skiing, and snowshoeing. *Convert anxiety, which is energy, into an activity that gives us a sense of achievement.* We should begin an exercise program gradually and have a doctor's checkup and possibly a stress test. We also want to be easy on ourselves as we increase our effort.

Stress is not a killer, only our reactions to stress. *Warning:* the first symptom of a heart attack, in 26 percent of cases, is instant death. This does not give us much time to change the way we deal with stress. The foundations of our lives are our health, vitality and physical well-being. Only by being in good physical condition can we enjoy our work and our loved ones.

Work

The second positive addiction is work. We can take our work home with us. Then, if we become irritable, we can get some work done. The job is not using us. Rather, we are using the job for a sense of achievement.

We solve the problem or deal with the stress that the problem creates. We adopt stress-relieving strategies to dissipate and channel this energy.

Relationships

The third positive addiction is relationships. We can ask our boss for advice, brainstorm with an associate, or counsel with a friend. We express our frustrations to a neighbor and have quality time with our family. We can also play out our feelings with someone we love.

Solitude

The fourth positive addiction is solitude. We can read a book, watch a sunset, play a musical instrument, meditate or engage in some spiritual activity. Many people have difficulty being alone. For them solitude translates into loneliness. We will all benefit from developing a relationship with ourselves. Such activities as internal dialogue, writing poetry, or canoeing on a lake can help us "become our own best friend," enhance our self-image and increase our self-respect.

We can be just as easily addicted to a positive activity as a negative one. All we need is ego strength to make the transfer from one to the other.

In the fall of 1968 I was teaching college in the morning and early afternoon and conducting corporate seminars from three until ten o'clock in the evening. I was having difficulty dealing with the pressure. In my efforts to reduce stress, I decided to minimize my long-distance running. In this way I would have more time and energy.

Soon I experienced more stress. I was having difficulty sleeping, and regardless of how much I had slept, I would often be tired. I also began experiencing a variety of minor physical ailments and had less energy. Somewhat in desperation I decided to increase the miles I was running. Soon I was sleeping and feeling better.

I discovered that if we are exhausted by stress we will sleep restlessly. We will not experience the deep sleep that restores energy, and when we awake, regardless of how much sleep we have had, we will still be tired. Exercise "burns" toxic energy and "clears" our mind.

Now I was able to handle more stress before becoming upset, more easily understand the causes of my frustration and make better decisions. I had more energy. I was also enjoying the opportunity to be alone and think without distraction. Exercising less to save energy can actually reduce energy.

Too often we allow toxic energy to erode our enthusiasm. Soon we may feel overwhelmed by the stress and become emotionally exhausted. Often the tension becomes the cork on the bottle of our positive emotions.

As an illustration, I can recall those evenings when I got home from work at IBM and felt exhausted. I wanted to run, but my body felt depleted of energy. The thought of making the effort seemed unreasonable. Yet, as a symbol of self-discipline, I would begin. Within a few miles, I felt exhilarated, and by the time I returned home, I was feeling good. The stress of the day had bottled up my positive energy. Physical activity "burns" the toxic energy first, so that our natural energy will rise within us and be released.

Channeling Stress

There is positive and negative energy. Positive energy is enthusiasm and originates from our desire to satisfy our needs. We feel the excitement of competing in a tournament, taking a vacation with someone we love or dealing with a fun part of our job. Negative energy develops when we are frustrated because we are not satisfying our needs.

Some of us merge our positive and negative energy together, as though two rivers of emotions merged into one. Often these currents of energy are turbulent and cause us to feel overanxious. Yet *this single river of energy can carry us through the obstacles that others avoid.*

If we allow negative energy to influence the way we feel, we might be unhappy and ineffective. There are two basic solutions. First, we can eliminate the causes of our negative energy.

First, we could

Change our attitude toward what is frustrating us

Decide the irritation is petty and disregard the problem

or

Resolve the conflict

Second, we can

Channel the negative energy into our river of enthusiasm

and

Create the overdrive that can assure our success

We could

Become absorbed in a productive activity

or

Confront the problem patiently until the obstacles in our path are eroded into stepping-stones

In life there are spectators and participants, just as there are in sports. We need to run the race, not watch it. There are those of us who enjoy the exhilaration of the effort and those who sit on the sidelines and observe. We want to feel the chill of the water in ocean swimming, the meditative mood while running through a meadow and the stimulation of backpacking along a crystal-clear lake.

Our physical activities, beyond keeping us in shape, should be pleasurable. Our job also should meet the two objectives, of helping us toward financial independence while being ego satisfying.

In relationships we also know people who enjoy their contact with others and those who sit on the sidelines. Many of us are reluctant to extend ourselves and develop intimacy with our closest relatives and friends. Rather, we convert the negative energy of our loneliness into such activities as watching television, playing golf or becoming a workaholic.

We want to live life with the exhilaration from exercise that stimulates us, the satisfaction of challenging work, and the passion of good relationships, rather than watching bowling on television or sleeping late.

Rick Barrett became a realtor in Malibu in 1978 and, two years later, sold me an acre of land on which I built my home. Rick is a well-balanced person, and his activities are for pleasure as well as relieving stress.

The real estate industry is notorious for being cyclical. The market was down in 1982, and while Rick continued to put time and energy into his business, he also became the president of the Malibu Board of Realtors.

Giving of my time to help other people helps me eliminate anxiety so that I can more easily stay focused on my objectives. During the down times I have taken on greater responsibility. In 1991, with the market down again, I coached two youth teams through the playoffs and stayed in a leadership position within the real estate association. Rather than crawling into a shell, I was able to take my mind off the difficult times through these community activities. For example, the big Malibu fire of 1978 burned me out. I had planted a thousand pine trees and lost almost all of them. Utter devastation. When times are difficult, I know I will make it. I just remind myself that if I persevere I will survive. If I keep my wits about me, I will deal with the reversals. With my wife and children to support me, the down cycles will only strengthen me for the next positive turn.

Malibu is vulnerable to catastrophic disaster: fires that travel on the wind at 70 mph, earthquakes that are frightening, storm tides that rip away the foundation of homes and mud slides that close down the roads and leave you isolated. But living life and living in Malibu are synonymous. While both are beautiful neither is for the timid of heart. We need the courage to persevere if we are going to enjoy all that life has to offer.

Positive outlets convert stressful situations into ego-satisfying activities.

Exercise helps us feel better by burning toxic energy and improving our health.

We seek responsibilities that give us a sense of purpose, so our work becomes a positive addiction.

Developing friendships that are supportive of our aspirations can help us persevere through periods of anxiety.

Seeking solitude during stressful periods can strengthen our self-sufficiency.

31
Three
Decisions

Capitalize on adversity, negative feedback and stress.

There are three decisions we need to make regarding failure, rejection and anxiety. First, we need to decide that there are no bad days. If ever again our life is not all we hoped it would be, we must realize what we have gained. Failure might not be as much fun as success, but it offers us many more benefits. We determine the benefits of failure.

Remember Buzz Aldrin, the astronaut who landed on the moon. Afterwards, he openly discussed the cause of his frustrations. When you have landed on the moon, what else is there? What is the next challenge or the next amusement? He could find nothing equally exciting. Our happiness depends on our continually evolving and reaching for new levels of success.

The second decision is to react to rejection with sensitivity. We rediscover the perfect child within us. We create, as in the martial art of jujitsu, the ability to disarm people when they attack us. Confrontation is part of our lives. People often become resistant and unreceptive to us. We do not avoid confrontation or overreact and become hostile. We react pleasantly. We become aggressively sensitive.

The last decision is to eliminate a negative and add a positive addiction. Review the list of negative addictions and decide which one you will eliminate. Then decide which of the four positives you will add or increase. If we discontinue a negative, but we do not add a positive, we might find ourselves gaining weight or becoming irritable. When we eliminate a negative, we have to either add or increase a positive to absorb, relieve and channel our anxiety into productive activities that assure our success.

Negative addictions, such as alcohol and tobacco, can make us feel good. However, the hangover the next morning, cirrhosis of the liver, or lung cancer are the results of our desire to feel good now without concern for how bad we may feel in the future.

Creating Energy

The main reason any of us take drugs, smoke or drink alcohol is because these substances make us feel the way we want to feel. The good feelings are brought on by chemical reactions that are temporarily created by the caffeine, nicotine, alcohol or any other addictive substances. Later, however, we are vulnerable to becoming more depressed or irritable.

Rather than being self-destructive, we must learn how to create the desired feelings through positive devices. For example, sensual fantasies can create sexual energy, meditation can cause us to feel very relaxed, a competitive sport can generate adrenal reactions, hypnosis can eliminate pain and aerobic exercise releases endorphins. We can program our minds to initiate any chemical or emotional reaction that we wish or disengage any we dislike.

No matter whether we are rich or poor, loved or lonely, most important is the way we feel. If we are rich, loved and famous, but we are depressed, then we are in an unfortunate situation. Conversely, if we are poor, alone and homeless, we can still be happy if we

Go for a long walk at sunset

Take an evening adult education class and develop our job skills

Listen to someone who is experiencing more difficulty and offer advice

Read a book in a library

The challenge is to manage our feelings. We can accomplish this by abandoning the negative addictions, which generate only false feelings of well-being and are self-destructive. Then we use positive addictions in a balance that makes us feel good.

There are two kinds of emotional pain. We experience one kind when we accept a challenge that is stressful. Those who stop smoking usually experience cravings and considerable emotional pain. Beginning an exercise program can cause even more stress.

However, the greatest emotional pain comes from thinking about confronting a stressful challenge. There are some of us, for example, who, when thinking about jogging, lie down until the thought goes away. Don't think about making the change. Just do it!

Eliminating a negative and adding a positive addiction can temporarily cause us more stress. However, if we stay consistent and persevere, eventually the cravings for the negative addiction will disappear, and we will *become addicted to the positive experience*. As an example, the first quarter mile in jogging might be painful, but soon a few miles become easy.

Four Factors for Happiness

If we achieve four objectives in life we will be happy:

1. Health—to experience energy, vitality and longevity

2. Financial success—to have the affluence that allows us to enjoy what we deserve

3. Love—to have someone who satisfies our needs for friendship, affection and intimacy

4. Peace of mind—to be our own best friend

Consider the relationships between these four objectives and the four positive addictions: We can improve our *health* by developing an exercise program. We do not have to enjoy exercise to appreciate the benefits of good health.

Our *financial success* comes from work. We do not have to enjoy every aspect of our work to enjoy the benefits of the money that our efforts create.

Love originates from relationships. By expressing our feelings and sharing thoughts, we create the friendships and romance that satisfy our needs for companionship and intimacy.

Peace of mind comes from solitude. As we enjoy being alone in activities that are avocational, meditative and spiritual, we develop a relationship with our self that helps us develop our potential, enhance our self-image and increase our self-esteem.

We must understand how our success in life is directly related to our ability to capitalize on failure and rejection. Yet failure and rejection are not as much the problem as the anxiety these experiences create.

We know that our ability to deal with stress is a primary factor for success in any risk-oriented challenge. If the thought of trying new ideas and exploring the unknown causes so much anxiety that we become defensive, then we may never achieve our expectations. However, if we thrive on anxiety, then stress will stimulate us to increase our effort.

Remember, we become the person we were designed to be when we have the courage to admit our frailties and the willingness to suffer through frustration.

We evaluate our attitude toward failure. We think about our perceptions of reality. We understand our expectations. Then we change our reactions.

Whenever people are hostile to us, we do not back off or overreact. Instead, we react pleasantly, disengaging their resistance until they become receptive to our suggestions.

Finally, we eliminate negative addictions and develop positive ways of channeling stress. We make these changes, not just to live longer and feel better, but for our own self-respect.

Those of us who live life to the fullest set high expectations. Once we succeed, we seek new challenges. When we confront defeat, we become stimulated and pursue the unknown. Rather than seeking security, we explore beyond the horizon where the outcome is unpredictable.

We find balance somewhere between being comfortable and living life dangerously. We want our past successes to create a secure foundation that allows us to feel comfortable in seeking the next level. Yet being too risk-oriented can cause us to raise the stakes too high so that we are in danger of losing all we have worked so hard to gain.

Realize how easily our satisfaction can evolve into comfortableness, boredom and depression. We want the mystery of extending ourselves into the unknown. We will each be successful when we have found the unique balance between the comfortableness of the predictable and the stimulation of the new.

In our society, most of us want to win the race, regardless of the pain. Too often the anxiety erodes our determination, and we think of discontinuing the effort. We feel overwhelmed, and we want to quit the race. If we look at those around us, we might realize that most everyone else is also struggling. So often after my lectures, people will tell me, "I thought I was the only one who was having difficulty with failure and rejection." We need to take away the stigma of defeat. The fear of failing plagues most everyone. We need to know that we are not the only ones who are experiencing difficult times.

In closing, I will quote from Theodore Roosevelt, who understood that winning and losing are not our concerns, but rather our ability to capitalize on whatever happens:

> Far better it is to dare mighty things, to win glorious triumphs, even though checkered by failure, than to take rank with those poor spirits who neither enjoy much nor suffer much, because they live in the gray twilight that knows not victory nor defeat.

Failure accelerates our success.

Rejection enhances our self-image.

Anxiety is an energy for positive momentum.

Index

Michelangelo, 12
Miller, Ann, 137
Momentum:
 negative, 16
 positive, 10, 19, 23, 141, 172
Morgan Stanley, 114
Motivation, 103, 109, 117, 125, 180
 and demotivators, 120
Murphy, Audie, 112
Murray, Bill, 23

Needs, 145–147, 150, 187
Negative feedback, 8, 13
 being programmed by, 10
 capitalizing on, 9
Nixon, Richard, 157, 158
Norton, Ed, 128

Objectivity, 97, 98, 100, 101, 140, 171, 175
Obsession, positive, 108

Paige, Satchel, 138
Park City, Utah, 123
Pasadena College, 20, 31
Patterns, establishment of successful,
 60–63
Peanuts, 142
Penicillin, 129
Perception, 101, 102, 110, 125, 167, 193
Performance, 115, 140–142, 150, 159, 161
Perseverance, 30, 100, 111, 122, 138, 142,
 153, 154, 158, 184, 188
Personality, 127, 128, 149, 150, 154, 157, 168
Perspective, 28, 137, 147, 172
Peter Principle, 109
Peterson, Donald E., 150
Physician Computer Network, 119
Potential, development of, 95, 104, 124,
 131, 155, 158, 168, 169, 192
Prayer of serenity, 174
Predators, 174
Presentation, 120, 134, 158, 170
Price Waterhouse, 137
Purpose, 171, 172

Rapport, 145–150
Reactions, 10, 110, 119, 121, 123, 128, 140,
 142, 143, 155, 157, 167, 180, 182, 185,
 191, 193
 to failure, 181

Reactions (*Cont.*):
 under pressure, 125, 126, 158
Reagan, Ronald, 157, 158
Receptivity, 146
Rejection, 6, 12, 13, 101, 104, 108–110, 113,
 114, 119, 120, 130, 136, 138, 154, 155,
 158–160, 167–169, 182, 190
 avoidance of, 5
 becoming immune to, 142
 capitalizing on, 117, 192
 dealing with, 10, 27
 fear of, 107, 111, 123, 134, 149, 169
 feelings of, 161
 frequency of, 9, 122–126, 144
 insulation from, 9
 personal, 113, 127, 131, 172
 strengthening of self-image and, 105
 understanding, 113–116
 vulnerability to, 118, 121
Relationships, 95, 108, 111, 114, 117–131,
 143, 145–151, 159, 169, 181, 188, 192
Release, 171
Resiliency, 95, 100, 103, 110, 131, 138, 139,
 141, 150, 152, 168
 increasng, 50–57
Resistance, 143
Results, 118, 120, 145, 147–150, 153, 175,
 178, 185
Risk, 108, 111, 124, 155, 159, 183, 192, 193
Risk taking, 81–88
Robinson, Jackie, 138
Rogers, Will, 104
Role playing, 152, 153
Roosevelt, Franklin D., 17
Roosevelt, Theodore, 131, 194

Sanders, George, 99
Self-esteem, 9, 99, 104, 131, 137
 increasing, 178, 192
 loss of, 113
 strengthening, 43–49
Self-image, 8, 117–120, 123, 127, 128, 130,
 137, 158, 169, 171
 enhancement of, 99, 103, 117, 131, 178,
 186, 192
 improvement of, 127–132
 raising of, 136
Self-reliance, 114
Self-respect, 138, 193
 increase in, 186